ANALOGIES:
A VISUAL APPROACH TO WRITING

ANALOGIES:
A VISUAL APPROACH TO WRITING

Anthony Garcia and Robert Myers

Professors of English, Rio Hondo College

McGraw-Hill Book Company

New York   St. Louis   San Francisco   Düsseldorf
Johannesburg   Kuala Lumpur   London   Mexico
Montreal   New Delhi   Panama   Paris   São Paulo
Singapore   Sydney   Tokyo   Toronto

To Kathy   To Monika

And for years of advice and encouragement,
our special thanks to Norman Lewis

Library of Congress Cataloging in Publication Data

Garcia, Anthony.
  Analogies: a visual approach to writing.

  1. English language—Rhetoric.   I. Myers, Robert,
date   joint author. II. Title.
PE1408.G27   808'.04275   74–1450
ISBN 0–07–022825–6

Analogies: A Visual Approach to Writing

1234567890MUMU7987654

This book was set in Baskerville by University Graphics, Inc. The editors were David Edwards and Susan Gamer; the designer was Elaine
M. Gongora; the production supervisor was Bill Greenwood. The drawings were done by Vantage Art, Inc.
The Murray Printing Company was printer and binder.

Cover Credits

Painting reproduced on front cover, lower right: Dali, Salvador. THE
PERSISTENCE OF MEMORY (Persistance de la memoire). 1931. Oil on
canvas, 9½ x 13″. Collection, The Museum of Modern Art, New York.

Painting reproduced on back cover, center: Van Doesburg, Theo.
(C.E.M. Kupper). COMPOSITION (THE COW). 1961. Gouache, 15⅝ x
22¾″. Collection, The Museum of Modern Art, New York.

CONTENTS

PREFACE

We hope to convince students that writing is fun and easier than they thought.

Despite the grumblings of many teachers, today's kids do not want to be spoon-fed. On the contrary, they are looking for an education in which they can be more personally active. Moreover, their disdain for the traditionalist's ever-narrowing conception of reality amounts to a healthy reaction, for all vital thought comes out of feeling. In the words of Abraham Maslow:

> If our hope is to describe the world fully, a place is necessary for pre-verbal, ineffable, metaphorical, primary-process, concrete-experience, intuitive, and esthetic types of cognition, for there are certain aspects of reality which can be cognized in no other way.*

But one-dimensional minds cannot teach people to be round. Nor can one-dimensional texts. Hence, our book.

We believe that the arts of communication can be taught only when intellect and social purpose are related to a student's own sensory awareness—the task that has always been the prime purpose of liberal education. Accordingly, our book begins with lessons and group experiences designed to make the student more aware of himself, giving him a perspective from which to write. Then we explore the connections between his view of the world and the language he uses and understands. We develop his confidence by showing him that verbal expression is not a special gift but an urge as common as walking or eating; and we stress the shaping power of his unconscious, which is the true source of all his thought, conscious logic being only the "afterthought." In addition, we show the significance for life and sanity of all forms of art—emphasizing the written forms—and consistently demonstrate our strictures with examples from the visual arts, in the light of evidence that we are all vastly more susceptible to visual persuasions than to any other kind. Indeed, since it has been estimated that today's average child has seen twenty feature films for every book he has read, we think it only common sense to work from visual familiars back to the related, but actually more complex, problems of writing.

*Toward a Psychology of Being, Princeton, 1962. Quoted in Richard Kean et al., Dialogue on Education, Bobbs-Merrill, Indianapolis, Ind., 1967.

GROUP ACTIVITIES

Although most of the lessons and related exercises in this book are designed for execution and evaluation in *small groups* (usually from four to six students seated together in a close circle), the greater part of this work *can* be conducted in the context of an entire class, if an instructor so chooses.

Anthony Garcia
Robert Myers

EXERCISES

Often an object that defies identification can be brought into focus by a mere word that classifies it. That word can serve as the key to the object's reality.

1.   Consider the objects shown in Figures 1-1a and 1-1b. What are they? Do they seem to have a function? Decide what that function might be and write it down (in a word or two) on the blank lines at the top of the opposite page.

Figure 1-1. Object *a. (Gabriele Wunderlich)*

Figure 1-1. Object *b. (Gabriele Wunderlich)*

chapter 1

I AM SIGNS, SYMBOLS, AND WORDS

We live in a world of *signs* and *symbols* and *words*. Because they are our keys to reality, words are the most important. In fact, it is often a word that communicates the meaning of a sign ("Stop") and a symbol ("Eden"). Not surprisingly then, the degree to which a civilization has successfully developed its ability to conceive complex ideas and abstractions is attributable to the wealth and sophistication of its language. The ancient Egyptians, for example, had no word for "freedom" in the sense we mean it today, and therefore they had no concept of it. A note on a piano exists only when we touch the key that strikes it; take away that key, and there is nothing. To an animal there is no sun or moon—there is only a physical sensation of light or warmth; cars or bicycles or bushes or boats or houses exist as things rather than concepts. In a sense we hardly exist ourselves when newly born and placed in a nursery basket. It is only when someone *names* us that we are fully there, and the name given us—whether Joe Doakes or Edward Kennedy—continutes to reinforce that "thereness" in a thousand ways.

As would-be writers, we are particularly concerned with words. Words are the pigments we squeeze out of a tube and mix on a palette and apply to a blank surface in order to say, "I think," "I feel," "I am." They are the minimum essential, for without them there are no sentences or paragraphs or books or plays or world views—no thoughts at all.

Without words to direct it, our modern world would soon become an incomprehensible maze of complexities. It would be impossible to give the simplest directions—to call a cab and direct it to our destination. It would be more than impossible to explain the difference between steel and iron and why they both rust, or to coordinate the machinery of government. In other words, we could not exist as we do today. Society without a sophisticated vocabulary would regress and suffer the famines, diseases, inconveniences, and superstitions of a primitive people.

To be comprehensible, our complex environment must be reduced to classifications. The Yellow Pages of the telephone book are an example of one of the countless efforts to do so. Since words are the vehicles with which this classification is accomplished, it is easy to see them as our keys to reality.

PART 1

Figure 1-1*a* _____

Figure 1-1*b* _____

2.   Now defend your decision by explaining why each of these objects is well designed to serve its function as you have identified it.

a. _____

_____

_____

_____

b. _____

_____

_____

_____

DISCUSSION: Compare your interpretation of these objects and their functions with those of your group members.

3.   For the solution to this puzzle, turn to page 46 (Figures 1-13 and 1-14). And now, with these correct identifications in mind, describe object *a* again on the following lines:

_____

_____

_____

_____

4.   Look at object *b* and then decide which *one* of the following phrases describes it most accurately. Indicate your choice by underlining the phrase.
    a. A utilitarian piece of art
    b. A commonly shaped wineglass
    c. A beautiful goblet

d. A wineglass

e. An artistic achievement

f. A simply sculptured wineglass

g. A wineglass of modern design

DISCUSSION: Compare your revised estimates of objects *a* and *b*. Once these objects were identified, was it easier to describe them? Consider how each exercise demonstrated that words are our keys to reality.

WORDS—MIRRORS OF OUR MINDS

Words are more than letters combined to make sounds. They are the vehicles by which the complex sensations we call thoughts and feelings are communicated. A child's language is imprecise because he has not yet fathomed the subtle degrees and differences between the sensations he experiences. The feelings he classifies as "love" ("Tell Mommy you love her"), he will eventually reclassify as one of the many more specific kinds of affection: attachment, admiration, esteem, regard, infatuation, or idolatry.

When a sensation becomes a word, thought is born. The more precise the word that reflects the sensation, the more precise the thought. And ultimately the sensation and the word are inseparable. Furthermore, if everyone has a unique sensibility, it should follow that everyone's language patterns are unique. Linguistic studies have found this to be true. Cumulatively, a person's thinking patterns become a singular series of word groups that forms the basis for his style. A speech by Edward Kennedy is recognizable his style and not Billy Graham's, and the style of *The Catcher in the Rye* is clearly distinct from that of *Jonathan Livingston Seagull*.

So in order to develop a good foundation for writing, you must explore your thoughts in depth and learn to distinguish your feelings with greater subtlety than ever before.

EXERCISES

It is seldom that we stand back and assess our feelings and preferences and prejudices. However, in this exercise you will be asked to do just that. And after you have come to some conclusions about yourself, compare your findings with those of others.

1. After each of the following questions there is a series of possible answers. Choose the best answer in each series by placing a check in the adjoining box.

    Question: How would you characterize yourself?

    a

    ☐ Romantic

    ☐ Realistic

    b

    ☐ Outgoing

    ☐ Aggressive

- ☐ Somewhat cynical
- ☐ A combination of the above

c
- ☐ A reserved conversationalist
- ☐ An enthusiastic conversationalist
- ☐ A witty conversationalist
- ☐ A poor conversationalist

e
- ☐ Satisfied with the present
- ☐ Unsatisfied with the present
- ☐ Satisfied with the present but eager to get on
- ☐ Unsatisfied but unsure about the future

Question: Which of the following would you prefer?

g
- ☐ An intimate discussion
- ☐ A heated discussion
- ☐ A reflective moment
- ☐ A group discussion

i
- ☐ Rock music
- ☐ Light opera
- ☐ Classical music
- ☐ A wide range of music

k
- ☐ Luxury
- ☐ Comfort
- ☐ Togetherness
- ☐ Simplicity

m
- ☐ An activity involving a few people
- ☐ An activity involving two
- ☐ An activity involving many
- ☐ Solitude

o
- ☐ A flashy car
- ☐ A well-engineered car
- ☐ A fast car
- ☐ A luxurious car

- ☐ Apathetic
- ☐ Introverted

d
- ☐ Easygoing
- ☐ Timid
- ☐ Forward
- ☐ Seductive

f
- ☐ Ambitious
- ☐ Driving
- ☐ Reserved
- ☐ Content

h
- ☐ Casual clothes
- ☐ "Far-out" clothes
- ☐ Conservative clothes
- ☐ "Sexy" clothes

j
- ☐ Structured activity
- ☐ Fun
- ☐ Leisure
- ☐ Solitude

l
- ☐ An intelligent date
- ☐ A sensitive date
- ☐ A charming date
- ☐ A sexy date

n
- ☐ A realistic novel
- ☐ A "message" novel
- ☐ An "action" novel
- ☐ A romantic novel

p
- ☐ A romantic dinner
- ☐ A walk along the beach
- ☐ A motorcycle ride
- ☐ Companionship

2.   Analyze your answers to the preceding questionnaire and establish a personality profile of yourself. Specifically, write two paragraphs on a blank sheet of paper. In the first paragraph, describe what you are. In the second, describe what you are not.

3.   Figures 1-2a to 1-2i show various activities. In the blanks that follow the pictures, identify each picture in your order of preference and give reasons for your choices.

ORDER OF PREFERENCE   REASON FOR CHOICE

_____   _____

_____   _____

_____   _____

_____   _____

_____   _____

_____   _____

_____   _____

_____   _____

a

c (A. Lopez–Omikron)

b (E. Baitel–Omikron)

d (A. Lopez–Omikron)

Figure 1-2

4.   Now describe the logical relationship, if any, between the personality profile you formulated in exercises 1 and 2 and the order of preference that you established in exercise 3 for the pictures of activities. Give reasons for your answers.

_____

_____

_____

_____

_____

_____

DISCUSSION: Within your group compare your answers to exercises 1, 2, 3, and 4. What differences do you note, and how can you account for these differences?

e (Gabriele Wunderlich)

h (A. Lopez–Omikron)

f   g

i

a

b

c

d

e

Figure 1-3

SIGNS AND SYMBOLS—OTHER MIRRORS

Although words are by far the most extensive method by which we communicate our thoughts, others exist. We communicate something about how we think, for example, by the way we dress (Figure 1-3a); by our many gestures (Figure 1-3b); or by our identification with a cause, a political party, or a religion (Figures 1-3c, d, and e).

The methods other than words by which we communicate our thoughts can be divided into two classifications, the sign and the symbol. Poor communication often occurs when these distinctions are not understood.

The Sign

A sign shows the existence of a thing, event, or condition in the past, present, or future. For example, smoke is a sign of fire, a skid mark on the pavement is a sign that a car has attempted to stop or has accelerated too fast, a red hexagon with "STOP" printed in the center is a sign that a condition for which one must stop exists, and a wink from a young man watching a girl pass by is a sign that he approves of what he sees. The message of a sign is characteristically straightforward and has a simple and predictable meaning. Because of these characteristics, signs are useful primarily because they communicate immediately. In fact, our reaction to them is often a matter of reflex rather than reasoning. Many of us occasionally drive our cars in a semiconscious dream state yet are able to obey the many traffic signs that guide us along our way.

The Symbol

A symbol suggests that a thing, event, or condition in the past, present, or future has a complex meaning beyond the literal (the sign). For example, the dollar sign ($) literally means a specific currency; as a symbol, however, it can represent materialism, corruption, a goal in life, or pleasure. Some symbols have a basic meaning, understood by all, as does the raised fist when it represents solidarity; however, a meaning broadened by personal prejudices usually goes beyond that understood by everyone. (The seemingly simple image of a school bus, for example, suggests many symbolic meanings: forced integration, justice, equality, youth, tax expenditures, happy days, drudgery, etc.)

EXERCISES

After looking at Figures 1-4a through 1-4d (page 12), do the exercises that follow.

1. Determine the drawings' signs.

    a. _____

    _____

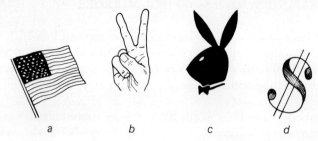

a   b   c   d

Figure 1-4

b. _____

_____

c. _____

_____

d. _____

_____

2.   Determine the drawings' symbolic meanings.

a. _____

_____

b. _____

_____

c. _____

_____

d. _____

_____

3.   Tell how you feel about what each drawing represents.

a. _____

b. _____

_____

_____

c. _____

_____

_____

d. _____

_____

_____

4. Is a feeling about something a good key to understanding what it symbolizes? Explain.

_____

_____

_____

_____

_____

DISCUSSION: (1) In a small group, compare your own answers with those of others. Are they similar or different? Why? (2) Now try to imagine the varied scenes depicted below and discuss how you would react.

Does this reveal more about symbolism?
a. A businessman giving you the peace sign
b. Your mother visiting a Playboy Club
c. A teen-ager owning a new Cadillac
d. Your father driving a Volkswagen bus painted like an American Flag

SIGNS IN EVERDAY LIFE

Signs abound in everyday life. Body language is, by far, the most complex, the most interesting, and the most utilized of all signs. A secretary, for example, uses her knowledge of body language to decipher the varied moods of her boss. When he hits the desk with his fist, she knows he is angry; when he crosses his arms, she knows he is upset; when he smiles, she knows he is pleased with her work. There are phrases that have given corporal expressions meaning: "his jaw dropped," "his eyes opened wide," "his nose was in the air." The word "supercilious," which in Latin means a raised eyebrow, denotes snobbishness in English.

We give our feelings away by the way we walk, the way we smile, the intensity in our eyes, or the intonation in our voice. Since it is often by these signs alone that we judge or are judged by others, signs constitute an important medium of communication.

According to the book *Body Language,* by Julius Fast (M. Evans and Company, Philadelphia, 1970), interpersonal relations are facilitated if one can recognize the messages communicated by various parts of another person's body. Social distance (three feet) is the distance that separates people comfortably. To enter within three feet is considered a violation of privacy and a social taboo. However, if the signs from someone are right—where the hands are placed, how the cigarette is held, and how the legs are positioned while the person is sitting, to name only a few—that person has invited you to enter his or her area of privacy.

Whether body language is actually this precise is a matter of conjecture. That it does communicate feelings, however imprecisely, is indisputable. This alone is cause for sensitizing oneself more than just superficially to the uses and meanings of body language.

There is a danger of our stereotyping people by the signs we observe them displaying or of rejecting them because we misinterpret those signs. We should always be aware of this danger by realizing that many signs are at best awkward communicators and are subject to greater misinterpretation than words.

EXERCISES

Look at the people in Figures 1-5a to 1-5j. Attempt to determine something about their personalities as you see them by answering the questions that follow. Give reasons for your answers. (Write your answers in the spaces provided.)

1.   What does each seem to be thinking?

   a. _____

   _____

   _____

Figure 1-5

a (E. Baitel–Omikron)

b (E. Baitel–Omikron)

c (E. Baitel–Omikron)

e (A. Lopez–Omikron)

d (E. Baitel–Omikron)

f (A. Lopez–Omikron)

h (A. Lopez–Omikron)

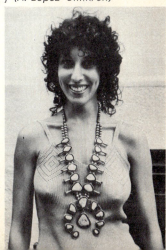

i (A. Lopez–Omikron)

j (A. Lopez–Omikron)

g (A. Lopez–Omikron)

b. _____

_____

_____

c. _____

_____

_____

d. _____

_____

_____

e. _____

_____

_____

f. _____

_____

_____

g. _____

_____

_____

h. _____

_____

_____

i. _____

j. _____

2. What would each consider to be a successful life?

a. _____

b. _____

c. _____

d. _____

e. _____

f. _____

g. _____

h. _____

i. _____

j. _____

3.   On a date where would each prefer to go?

a. _____

b. _____

c. _____

_d._ _____

_e._ _____

_f._ _____

_g._ _____

_h._ _____

_i._ _____

_j._ _____

_____

4. What make of car would each prefer to drive?

   a. _____

   _____

   _____

   b. _____

   _____

   _____

   c. _____

   _____

   _____

   d. _____

   _____

   _____

   e. _____

   _____

   _____

   f. _____

   _____

   _____

   g. _____

   _____

h. _____

_____

_____

i. _____

_____

_____

j. _____

_____

_____

5.   What would the bedroom of each look like?

a. _____

_____

_____

b. _____

_____

_____

c. _____

_____

_____

d. _____

_____

e. _____

_____

_____

f. _____

_____

_____

g. _____

_____

_____

h. _____

_____

_____

i. _____

_____

_____

j. _____

_____

_____

6.   How would each react to the drawings in Figures 1-4*a* through 1-4*d*?

a. _____

_____

b. _____

c. _____

d. _____

e. _____

f. _____

g. _____

h. _____

i. _____

_____

_____

j. _____

_____

_____

7.   Describe the type of novel each would be interested in reading.

a. _____

_____

_____

b. _____

_____

_____

c. _____

_____

_____

d. _____

_____

_____

e. _____

_____

_____

f. _____

_____

_____

g. _____

_____

_____

h. _____

_____

_____

i. _____

_____

_____

j. _____

_____

_____

8.   What characteristic of each seems most to influence your attitude toward him or her?

a. _____

_____

_____

b. _____

_____

c. _____

_____

_____

d. _____

_____

_____

e. _____

_____

_____

f. _____

_____

_____

g. _____

_____

_____

h. _____

_____

_____

i. _____

_____

_____

j. _____

_____

_____

DISCUSSION: (1) Compare and discuss your answers. Are these answers valid or are they wild guessing? (2) Do you consider your answers stereotypical? If so, is this justifiable? (3) Do your answers say something about you?

OPTIONAL EXERCISES

Choose someone in the class with whom you are not familiar. Do not speak to this person once you have made your selection. After observing this person, attempt to determine his or her personality as you see it by answering the following questions and giving reasons for them. Once you have done this, determine your own personality by answering the questions the way you think someone would see you.

1. Analysis of partner
    a. What would his (her) best friend be like? _____

    _____

    _____

    _____

    b. What type of novel would he (she) like to read? _____

    _____

    _____

    _____

    c. What make of car would he (she) prefer to drive? _____

    _____

    _____

    _____

d. What would be his (her) reaction to each drawing in Figure 1-4? _____

_____

_____

_____

e. What would he (she) consider to be his (her) greatest success? _____

_____

_____

_____

f. If he (she) were given a chance to visit any place in the world, where would it be?

_____

_____

_____

g. Where would he (she) go for an ideal date? _____

_____

_____

_____

h. What would he (she) buy if given $5,000? _____

_____

_____

_____

i. What would he (she) consider an ideal neighborhood? _____

_____

_____

_____

j. What would his (her) dream house be like? _____

_____

_____

_____

2. Self-analysis

a. _____

_____

_____

_____

b. _____

_____

_____

_____

c. _____

_____

_____

_____

d. _____

_____

_____

e. _____

_____

_____

_____

f. _____

_____

_____

_____

g. _____

_____

_____

_____

h. _____

_____

_____

_____

i. _____

_____

_____

_____

j. _____

_____

_____

_____

DISCUSSION: Now read your answers to your partner. How did your analysis of yourself match with your partner's analysis of you and vice versa?

LOOKING IN REVERSE

Novelists often choose to describe a character in general rather than specific terms. This forces the reader to fill in his own details and essentially create the image of the character for himself. We can call this image an "ideal" since it best fits the particular situation. Such a definition is implicit in the phrases "an ideal wife," "an ideal profession," and "an ideal speech."

Ideals are considered symbols rather than signs because they reflect all the unique experiences and feelings that each individual has learned to associate with them.

EXERCISES

The following passage from Balzac's novel *Pere Goriot* describes one of his female characters. It gives us a few concrete facts about her—she has just taken a bath, she is wearing cashmere attire with a low-cut neckline, she is wearing slippers, she has a small waist. Other than this, his description appeals to the ideal we have invested in such words and phrases as, "coquettish," "beauty," "voluptuous," "glamour," "freshness," "call to love," and "pretty." Read the passage below and answer the questions that follow.

Eugene turned quickly round and saw her, coquettishly dressed in a white cashmere wrap. . . . A perfume seemed to emanate from her; she had doubtless just come from her bath, and her beauty, thus softened as it were, seemed more voluptuous. Her eyes were moist. A young man's gaze misses nothing; it takes in a woman's glamour as a plant takes in its needed sustenance from the air. Eugene could feel the freshness of her hands without even touching them. Her neck was a call to love, and he saw, through the cashmere, the . . . curve of her breast, which the loose folds of her wrap left partly uncovered. His eyes lingered there. The countess had no need of a corset, and only a belt emphasized the slimness of her waist. Her slippered feet were very pretty.*

*Honore de Balzac, *Père Goriot*, trans. E. K. Brown, Dorothea Walter, and John Watkins. Copyright 1946, 1950 by Random House, Inc.

1.   If the author appeals to the ideal of the reader, does he communicate his own ideal?

     _____

     _____

     _____

     _____

     _____

2.   What would be the advantage of an author's appealing to the reader's ideal in a

     sketchy description rather than completing the description himself? _____

     _____

     _____

     _____

3.   As a reader you were forced to construct your own ideal picture of the character
     in question. Which of the women in Figures 1-5a to 1-5j comes closest to this
     ideal? Give reasons for your answers. _____

     _____

     _____

     _____

     _____

     DISCUSSION: Read and discuss your answers in groups.

SETTING—ANOTHER SIGN

Isolated, a facial expression can be very ambiguous. When placed in a setting, however, its meaning usually becomes more evident. This is true because setting can
function as a sign and as such conveys information—in this case, information
necessary to clarify the meaning of the facial expression. The setting of an old,

dilapidated shack, for example, is a sign of poverty, and a facial expression seen within this setting can be judged in accordance with the meaning of this setting.

In later chapters we will see that it is also often important in writing to depict our characters in the exact situation in which they are seen since the situation also has meaning and can be a clue to understanding the characters. The importance of setting in the analysis of character is exemplified in the following exercises.

Figure 1-6 *(Omikron)*

EXERCISES

Look at Figure 1-6.

1. In the following space, analyze the character and describe him. Attempt to determine the reason for his expression by imagining him in a setting in which you might expect to find him. Attempt to give as much detail about this imagined

    setting as possible. _____

    _____

    _____

    _____

    _____

    _____

    _____

2.   When this is done, turn to Figure 1-12 (page 46) to find the character in the actual context or setting from which he was taken originally. Answer the following questions in the space given.

   a. Does the character now seem to be expressing the same feelings that you first decided he was? _____

   _____

   _____

   b. Is the context similar to the one you imagined? _____

   _____

   _____

   c. How has the context influenced your interpretation of the meaning of the character's expression? _____

   _____

   _____

3.   Rewrite your description in the following blanks using the actual setting as your qualifier. _____

   _____

   _____

   _____

   _____

   _____

CREATING SYMBOLS

We all have memories of the past—some pleasant, some unpleasant, but all, nevertheless, integral parts of our lives. Many of these memories we have condensed into symbols and stored economically in the subconscious. For example, we may have condensed memories of someone we love and the times we have spent together into a certain song; or we may have condensed a flood of happy or sad associations into the image of an old car we have had in the past; or visiting our old neighborhood, we may find that we have condensed memories of our youth into that neighborhood.

These symbols are characteristically very personal. Therefore, when we refer to personal symbols in our speaking or writing, we must take great care to explain their significance. This must be done if we are to communicate the context into which we have put these symbols.

Occasionally, after being introduced to someone and conversing with them, we are told that we would have found what they said more meaningful if we had known them better. What we are being told is that we failed to understand the symbolic meaning behind that person's statements.

If we speak or write, and therefore communicate, poorly, it is often because we have failed to clarify our unique associations.

When we create symbols, we "synthesize" (draw together) all our associations with something into words, signs, or objects. We "abstract" those associations; that is, we try to find something that conveys the essence of those associations. For example, we refer to the office of a king as the "crown," or we often hear something unoriginal referred to as "middle-class." Abstracting reality is also one of the basic methods of modern art and is one of the reasons it is referred to as "abstract art."

Maxim:
The more something is abstracted, the more general, obscure, and symbolic it becomes and correspondingly the more difficult to interpret or explain.

EXERCISES

In Figures 1-7a to 1-7d four students drew their conceptions of the world. Each drawing, from the first to the last, becomes more abstract and correspondingly more difficult to interpret.

The next series of drawings, Figures 1-8a to e, by the well-known artist Van Doesburg, shows an increasing degree of abstraction. If applied in this case, would the maxim above hold true? Explain.

_____

_____

_____

a

b (Margie Naumann)

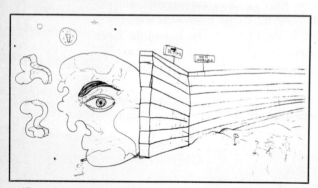

c (Fred Graham)

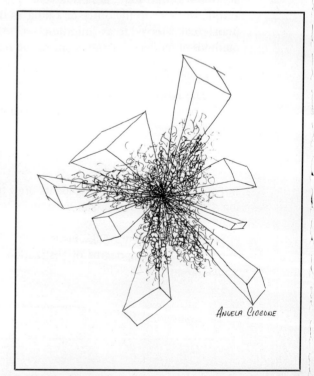

d (Angela Ciccone)

Figure 1-7

a b c

a, b, and *c.* Theo Van Duesburg (C. E. M. Kupper), three of eight studies for *Composition (The Cow),* pencil (each 4⅝ x 6¼ in.), n.d. Collection, The Museum of Modern Art, New York.

e Theo Van Duesburg (C. E. M. Kupper), *Composition (The Cow),* oil on canvas (14¾ x 25 in.), 1916–1917. Collection, The Museum of Modern Art, New York.

d Theo Van Duesburg (C. E. M. Kupper), *Composition (The Cow),* gouache (15⅝ x 22¾ in.), 1916. Collection, The Museum of Modern Art, New York.

Figure 1-8

Figure 1-9 Salvador Dali, *The Persistence of Memory (Persistence de la Memoire),* oil on canvas (9½ x 13 in.), 1913. Collection, The Museum of Modern Art, New York.

1. On a blank piece of paper draw a picture which you feel represents (symbolizes) your relationship to the class. On another piece of paper draw a picture that represents your feelings about America. Choose a one-word title for each.

2. On the same or another piece of paper write a detailed explanation of both pictures. Be sure to explain all the relationships that occur within each picture.

3. The painting by Dali shown in Figure 1-9 symbolizes his concept of time as your own drawing symbolizes your feelings about America. With this in mind, explain this painting as you explained your own picture (on a separate sheet of paper).

DISCUSSION: (1) Show your pictures to the members of your group. Each member will give an explanation of a picture after giving it a title. Do the titles also symbolize the picture's meaning? (2) Compare your explanations of Dali's painting. Choose the most plausible explanation, which should be read to the entire class.

ADVERTISING—CREATING SYMBOLS

The ultimate goal of advertising is successful sales. The immediate goals are to inform consumers of a product and to establish that product as a recognizable symbol. Because we are studying symbolism, the last goal deserves our attention.

The first immediate goal of advertising, *informing consumers,* is praiseworthy because it stimulates the economy and makes people aware of the various facilities and mechanisms available for their personal comfort and enjoyment. The second immediate goal, *creating symbols,* is a questionable practice because it encourages stereotyping (a Cadillac represents success) and appeals to the vanity rather than the real needs of the consumer. It creates a psychological dependency (the need for a mouthwash) with behavioral techniques and establishes "plastic" priorities and distorted criteria for gauging the success of one's endeavors.

The following are specific charges leveled against advertising by its critics: (1) it creates symbolic illusions, (2) it programs feelings, (3) it builds false hopes and tends to standardize our sensitivities, and (4) it gives sex an inordinate priority in our lives by suggestion.

In the following exercises you will be asked to analyze three advertisements (Figures 1-10*a* to 1-10*c*) and decide for yourself if the charges of the critics are valid. Then you will be asked to decipher the mechanics involved in making the products advertised symbolic.

EXERCISES

1. In the following blanks, state whether you agree or disagree with the criticisms leveled against advertising. Support your opinions with specific examples.

    _____

    _____

    _____

    _____

    _____

    _____

2. After looking at the advertisements (Figures 1-10a to 1-10c), determine the symbolic meanings they have created for their products.

a

b

c

Figure 1-10

a. _____

_____

_____

b. _____

_____

_____

c. _____

_____

_____

3.   Explain the mechanics by which the products advertised in Figures 1-10a to 1-10c have been made symbolic.

a. _____

_____

_____

b. _____

_____

_____

c. _____

_____

_____

4.   Do the criticisms leveled against advertising apply to Figures 1-10a to 1-10c? Support your opinion.

_____

_____

_____

_____

_____

DISCUSSION: Discuss your answers in groups of three or four and see if you can reach a position statement concerning the creation of symbols by advertising.

MIX-UP OF SYMBOLS = MISUNDERSTANDING

As we have seen thus far, symbolism is widely used in our communications systems. Since symbols are products of our individual associations and since our associations are so varied, there is a good possibility of misinterpretation when we communicate with them.

The following article from *Time,* depicting the varied reactions to the drawing of a nude man and woman which was sent aloft on the spacecraft *Pioneer 10* (see Figure 2-2a, page 53), exemplifies such misinteruretations.

RORSCHACH IN SPACE

When astronomers Frank Drake and Carl Sagan conceived the idea of attaching a drawing of a nude man and woman to the *Pioneer 10* spacecraft, their motive was purely scientific. They wanted any extraterrestrial beings who might some day intercept the craft to know what kind of race had sent it. Since the March launch, however, the two scientists have discovered that the drawing is more than a message to outer space. "We didn't realize it," says Drake, "but it turns out to be a cleverly disguised Rorschach ink-blot test."

In the Rorschach, people reveal their emotional conflicts by describing what they think they see in indeterminate shapes. Similarly, critics of the *Pioneer 10* drawing saw considerably more than Drake and Sagan intended to convey, thus suggesting something about their own inner preoccupations.

One citizen interpreted the man's upraised arm as a Nazi salute. The same assertive gesture, in addition to the man's taller stature, was interpreted by militant women as male chauvinism. Actually, the male's position was intended to show how the human arm moves and to display man's fingers and opposed thumb. The woman's stance demonstrates not passivity but the workings of the hip. Also, Drake observes, most men really are taller than most women.

One group complained that the figures were "obviously" white; another claimed they were "obviously" black. The truth, says Artist Linda Sagan (Carl's wife), is that she intended to show the man as Negro and the woman as Oriental, thus portraying diverse racial characteristics.

The complaints about pornography may well come from those who are uneasy about sexual differences. Anticipating such uneasiness (or perhaps betraying their own), some editors censored the picture, erasing the male genitals and the female nipples. Others printed the original drawing—and were blasted for purveying "filth." No one seemed satisfied; some faulted the unretouched drawing because it does not show the female genitalia. "We did think about showing the woman giving birth," Drake told a *Wall Street Journal* reporter last week, "but that would really have complicated things."*

In the following exercises, you will be asked to determine if the "Dear Abby" letter is a misinterpretation of symbols.

EXERCISES

Read the letter below and answer the subsequent questions.

"Her Poem Turns Off Teacher," by Abigail Van Buren

Dear Abby: I am 17 years old and enrolled in a creative writing course at school. My main purpose in taking this course was to get courage to express my feelings. I have been writing all my life, but have never shown anyone my work. Well, I loved this course as well as the teacher. He was one of the nicest men I have ever known. One day I expressed my feelings in the form of a poem and gave it to him. It went like this: "I dreamed you were my father. This dream did make me weep. I dreamed you were my father. My love for you runs deep. I dreamed you held me in your arms. And told me I was good. I dreamed that you would punish me. Each time you thought you should. I dreamed you were my father. This dream did make me weep. I dreamed you were my father. Though I was not asleep." I never had a father, and in this poem I was trying to tell my teacher how much he meant to me. Well, after he read it, he never even looked at me again. He won't call on me in class,

---

*"Rorscharch in Space," *Time,* June 5, 1972, p. 60. Reprinted by permission from TIME, The Weekly Newsmagazine; Copyright Time Inc.

and he turns his head when he sees me in the hall. I feel so embarrassed and ashamed. I don't want to go to his class any more, and I don't think I will ever show my work to anyone again. Was it corny of me to have expressed my feelings in poetry? I hate being rejected, and believe me, I've been rejected a lot.

Hurt

Dear Hurt: I think your poem was good, and I urge you not to let this unfortunate experience discourage you from writing, and sharing your work with others. Your teacher appears to be strangely insensitive for one who teaches creative writing. He cannot be expected to know the battles you are fighting in your personal life. (And you, nothing of the battles he could be fighting in his.) The feelings you expressed obviously turned him off. But I think he was more frightened than displeased.*

1. If we can assume that the reaction of the teacher is as indicated by the student above, is there a possibility that the different symbolic meanings that each associates with the word "father" might be the cause of their misunderstanding? If so, explain in the spaces below what these differences are. If you do not think that this is the problem, explain why and indicate what you think the problem is.

_____

_____

_____

_____

_____

_____

2. What should the student have added to or omitted from her poem in order to clarify her feelings?

_____

_____

_____

*Abigail Van Buren, "Dear Abby," *Los Angeles Times,* December 13, 1970, sec. F, p. 7.

3.   Do you agree with the reply to the letter? If you do, indicate why. If you do not,

how would you have replied?_____

_____

_____

_____

_____

_____

DISCUSSION: Compare answers and defend your position.

CONCLUDING STATEMENT

When we write, we distill our observations of the world into words, signs, and symbols. In this process we are relaying information that we have received from one medium through another. The difficulties of such a task lie in the fact that each medium has different strengths and weaknesses. With words, for example, we cannot relate something as precisely as we saw it. On the other hand, only with words, can we define the significance of what we saw.

EXERCISE

Figure 1-11 *(Gabriele Wunderlich)*

The following letter was inspired by Figure 1-11, which became a symbol around which the ideas in the letter were developed. Read it and complete the exercise that follows.

Dear English Class of Fall 19___,

Many years have elapsed since each one of you walked away from our completed class as individuals, no longer members of the team that destiny assembled. These many years have dissipated the memory of the days we spent together. More often than not, in fact, my forgetful mind recalls not a classroom full of warm and enthusiastic bodies, but rather a cold, sterile recess of a room in some forgotten corner of time that emits neither life nor excitement, but only dark, damp echoes of past time.

It is not easy to like this room because the sounds of the wind make the silence louder, and silence inevitably says that one is alone. When I occasionally enter into this room, I look at the old, decayed desk in search of a scratched name or initial that might reawaken memories, but the etchings of passing time have gouged these mementoes too. Occasionally pieces of decayed paint chance to fall and stir life into this void, but they, too, quickly become part of life's memory.

I try to analyze the significance of the empty room, but my ego rejects such an attempt. I am now a lonely old man with old thoughts attempting to look back to other old thoughts for companions.

During the last forty years, I have seen life change and become what only the greatest pessimists projected. There are no longer schools where students might debate and eke their way to knowledge. Today, in their stead, we have knowledgebanks that employ unskilled nurses who inject knowledge via programmed chromosomal injections. Hence intellectual life is fed by stagnant knowledge which produces insipid intellectuals.

My fleeting memories of you are memories of a time when life was confused but exciting and alive, memories of happy times that lived with ideas that were still dreams.

However much I try, I cannot remember you individually, but whoever you are, I wish you the best despite the times.

Yours   truly,

Professor_____

1. On a separate sheet of paper write a reply to the letter. Use a particular picture of your choice as the symbol around which you build your ideas.

Figure 1-12 *(Omikron)*

Figure 1-13. Object *a (Gabriele Wunderlich)*

Figure 1-14. Object *b (Gabriele Wunderlich)*

Answers to puzzle on page 5:
     Figure 1-1*a* is an electric light bulb
     Figure 1-1*b* is a wine goblet

chapter 2

I AM EXPRESSIVE

You have explored three essential elements for self-expression: signs, symbols, and words. You will now encounter the fourth and most important element: *self-confidence*. It is important because it is the force that ultimately propels you to weave the other three into a coherent, rhythmic, and decisive whole.

Success expressing yourself and the confidence to do so are "symbiotic"; that is, one depends upon the other for its existence—success develops confidence, and confidence stimulates success. This is problematic for the beginning writer because the success that he enjoys with each effort at writing at this early level is usually modest, obscure, and easy to misinterpret as a failure. It is understandably difficult to build confidence on such an apparently weak foundation. Because of this, it is best initially to eliminate traditional writing goals (as in this chapter) and thereby minimize any possibility of failure.

The following exercises are excellent opportunities to "toy" with words and ideas. They are intended to let the mind run free, unencumbered by the rules we usually associate with the written composition. They are the first steps in a process that will uncover how much you have to say and how great your potential is to say it.

EXERCISES

1. In this exercise, the class is asked to tell a continuous story. Someone will be chosen to begin it; then others will be chosen at random by the teacher or a student to continue where the previous person left off.

2. The instructions are the same as those of the previous exercise except that the stories will be told in groups of five or six (with someone in the group acting as moderator) and will be developed from the following sentences.
    a. The wheels screeched; suddenly there was an explosion and the crowd became silent.
    b. Everyone agreed that she was a mysterious woman who had changed the neighborhood since she moved in.
    c. Even until yesterday I had had the chance; however, now it was lost because of a foolish mistake.

    d. The family was always in a crisis, but Joe always bailed it out.

    e. Mike always leveled with Jim, his best friend; however, this time he couldn't bring himself to do it.

3.   The intent of this exercise is the same as that in the previous exercises: let your mind wander. You are to *write* for fifteen minutes whatever comes to your head. Do not stop writing at any time. If you get stuck, write down anything at all, non-sense or the same word over and over, until you can regroup your thoughts. Punctuation, correct spelling, and deliberate organization should be ignored if they interrupt your train of thought.

VISUAL ART—ANOTHER WAY TO SEE HOW YOU WRITE

For years, psychologists have noted correlations between a person's artistic expression and his psychological state. Recently, psycholinguists have found similar correlations between a person's psychological state and his writing. This need not be surprising when one considers that both writing and visual art are forms of self-expression.

Because of the similarities between visual art and writing, to build an analogy between the two to illustrate or clarify a point is valid and valuable. In lieu of this, we will discuss the improvement of a young man, Michael, as an artist and show how the steps he took to achieve success have their parallels in writing. We will particularly note that confidence and technical success are interrelated and that progress in one is reflected in the progress of the other.

Michael's success was self-motivated and was a reflection of the changes in his attitude toward himself. These changes were noted by those observing him. He improved rapidly as an artist considering that he had no technical direction.

We find his improvement from one drawing to another superficially very modest; however, we find the cumulative improvement from his first work (Figure 2-1*a*) to his last (Figure 2-1*b*) evidently dramatic when we compare them. If we were to

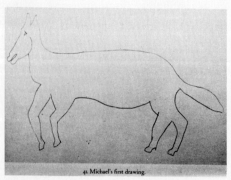

Figure 2-1*a*. Michael's first drawing.

Figure 2-1*b*. Michael's last drawing.

analyze a struggling writer's successive papers, we would note similar changes as his confidence became greater.

Michael's Story

Michael, at twenty, was a delinquent participating in an experimental program at a New York City reformatory. Initially, he appeared quiet, reserved, and indifferent. During his first art session he drew a horse (Figure 2-1a). He did not like this drawing but gave no reasons why. As an artistic rendition, it is a failure; however, it contains some elemental features of organization: (1) it is a total object with the main parts visualized (body, four legs, tail, and ears); (2) except for the jaw line, which partly covers the neck, no part interferes with another; and (3) the front and hind legs appear to be in a relationship of direction to one another, indicating the artist's elementary conception of motion.

The works of a writer still in the elementary stages of writing are analogous to this first drawing. These writings vaguely represent what the writer wants to say and because of their awkward phraseology and poor transitions are artistic failures. However, like Michael's first drawing, they form the bases for further improvement.

The second drawing (Figure 2-1c), "Horse Standing on Grass beside a Wooden Fence," represents a broader theme and indicates a greater interest on the part of the artist. Despite its awkwardness, it shows signs of improvement. For better comprehension, the artist has simplified the form to a rectangle to which the legs are attached singly and distinctly. In writing, simplification or basic outlining is likewise the first step necessary to bring a better perspective to the organization of an essay.

In his search for further clarification of his subject, Michael has achieved an even greater simplification in Figure 2-1d. This, however, has resulted in a stiffness of expression, particularly in the legs, which are no longer bent.

In Figure 2-1e, Michael is beginning to feel more confident and interested as reflected in his drawing and the statement he made about it: "I improved this last picture so much I cannot believe that I really done it, and I am going to make a whole herd of horses and colts by their mother and a king horse on a nearby hill."

Drawings subsequent to the fourth reflect Michael's ability to portray a more

Figure 2-1c. Michael's second drawing.

43. Michael's third drawing.

Figure 2-1d. Michael's third drawing.

three-dimensional figure and to overlap lines without breaking them. With each successive drawing he developed a more sophisticated ability to judge balance. This was evident in his disappointment over a later drawing in which the background foliage became overwhelming and obscured the horse, the intended focal point. He corrected this problem in Figure 2-1f his next drawing.

Figure 2-1e. Michael's fourth drawing.   Figure 2-1f. Michael's fifth drawing.

(2-1a through e originally published by the University of California Press; reprinted by permission of The Regents of the University of California.)

For five weeks, Michael became engulfed in the effort that produced Figure 2-1e. This drawing is the most artistic thus far and in its bold strokes displays a definite increase of inner security and a greater independence. In this drawing, Michael was able to achieve a better integration of the background foliage with the figure of the horse, although he was able to keep the latter dominant as was his intention. This he accomplished by regressing to an earlier period of order and simplicity, but this time blending the components of the drawing with a fluidity that comes only with artistry. This work led to the following comment by an observer:

> An evaluation of Michael's achievement as a work of art which not only attests to his mental accomplishment but also to his inner participation and to the change in him as a psychophysical whole—such an evaluation can be undertaken only by examining his work in relation to his own stage of development of visual conception. Any other consideration—such as comparison, in terms of naturalistic faithfulness to objects, with other works of art; or comparison of his work with work done on other artistic levels; or, as is common, evaluation by the standards of the observer's taste—cannot do justice to his production.
>
> Observation of his work on the basis of the pictorial data only leads to the following judgment. Both figures—horse and tree—became satisfactorily visible. In spite of overlappings, all essential features are clearly

shown. Any verbal explanation is superfluous. The figures can be distinctly recognized by observation only. The evolutionary process of creating the form of these figures has revealed that their structural organization is the result of Michael's visual conception and not of imitation of nature. In the construction of all forms, the stage of variability of direction is applied to all the main features; that is to say, parts are related to one another by similar angles. . . . The relationship between leaves and branches represents an earlier stage adopted in order to avoid confusion; and likewise with the lines of the hair in tail and mane. Furthermore, both figures are equally modeled. The most essential characteristics are realized. The figure of the horse, presented in its principal features, is placed against a background (tree) with more differentiated parts (leaves). This has the effect of a figure (horse) and a ground (tree) emphasizing each other in an interrelationship of form. But as the figure of the horse is the largest coherent unit in the picture, the not-so-coherent background serves to make the horse dominant in the subject matter. Form and content are thus indivisibly related. Finally, the picture reveals a uniformly applied relationship of variability of direction in all its parts. Even if the work is not a perfect unity of form, for an individual such as Michael . . . with extremely limited education and almost no opportunity for unfolding his inborn abilities, this work must be considered an extraordinary result.

    Michael's work required . . . a mental attitude that is characterized by intense unity in the function of all forces of visual conceiving: feeling, thought, will, and even physical concentration. This formative process, which involved his entire being, is organized mental activity of a high order. The organic unfolding of such energies may in turn lead to an increase of order and balance that are essential to the building of an integrated personality.

Michael's final project (refer back to Figure 2-1*b*) reflects a completely changed personality best described by the comments of an observer.

A glance at Michael's last work shows at once how much it differs from all previous efforts. The change in his behavior, from tense effort to relaxed, self-confident mastery of the artistic activity, is directly reflected in the striking difference between the comparatively rigid forms of the previous works and the ease of attitude and freely modulating form in this one. Its simplicity gives the relief its profound expression. . . . Head and lifted leg are in a relationship of direction to each other by which the movement of the leg does not become an isolated part, but belongs to the whole figure. All previously applied stages of Michael's visual conception are merged into an indivisible organization of form. The subtle oscillation in the outline of the body—from hinder back to middle back, to neck, to head—which recurs in the outline of the legs, gives a harmonious quality to the total picture.

The fluidity of expression in a completely configured form reflects a normal man with a developed sensitivity and a constructive mind. There are no longer any signs of "deep feelings of inferiority." There is a secure will which forms and builds up. There is no longer a lack of confidence that leads to timidity and passivity. Michael's last work is documentary evidence of a consummation of an inner change—a change from an "apparently immature youth" to the maturity of a newly awakened creative personality.*

The steps that led to Michael's final achievement parallel those necessary to achieve success as a beginning writer. As was the case in Michael's first drawing, the writer's first essay is often awkward and self-conscious. The sentences are characteristically short and disjointed and together form an obscured and confused message. As was the goal of Michael's second drawing, the goal of subsequent essays is greater simplicity by outlining. Once perspective is established by doing this, the basic focal point is broadened by further modification. This is analogous to the decorative foliage of Michael's later drawings. Finally, with greater understanding of mechanics and an increased interest generated by success, better transitions are developed between sentences, giving them a fluidity that they did not possess before. When these advancements are achieved, writing becomes peripherally "artistic."

In the following exercise, you will find two paragraphs that are roughly analogous to Figure 2-1*a* and 2-1*b* respectively. You will be asked to compare them.

EXERCISE

The second essay that follows is a development of the first one. On a separate piece of paper, explain in your own words why essay 2 is better than essay 1. Cite examples from both essays to prove your point.

1. WHY I SHOP AT SEARS

Sears is a big department store. A shopping center is next to the Sears store. I shop there, too. The parking lots are often empty. The store is very busy every night. I shop there because of the convenience.

2. WHY I SHOP AT SEARS

Large, nationally known department stores have become the hubs of huge

* Henry Schaefer-Simmern, *The Unfolding of Artistic Activity,* 1948. Originally published by the University of California Press; reprinted by permission of The Regents of the University of California.

shopping complexes in the last twenty years. Such a complex has been built in my area around Sears. This centralizes shopping and makes it convenient for me to satisfy the major part of my shopping needs in one stop.

The parking accommodations for our Sears and the adjoining shopping center are quite extensive and add to the customer's convenience. They are usually filled to near capacity in the evenings when the stores are the busiest, although they seem empty during the early morning and late afternoon hours.

When I consider the many conveniences Sears and the adjoining stores have to offer, I realize why I seldom shop elsewhere.

THE INFINITE VARIETIES OF AN IDEA

A horse is hardly a unique subject for a painting; however, Michael's final rendition of a horse is as uniquely his as his fingerprints. If you were to see it again, you would recognize it as his despite the countless drawings of horses that you might have encountered in the interim. It represents not only the development of a mechanical ability which might be standardized, but the probing for a form to express a vision that is unique.

The uniqueness of Michael's horse attests to the belief that a single idea harbors infinite possibilities for its development. Further proof of this lies in the distinctive differences between the following drawings rendered by different artists in response to this task: Communicate something about earthlings to extraterrestrial aliens (Figure 2-2a to c). Figure 2-2a, drawn by Linda Sagan (see page 41 for the complete story), was actually sent aloft with the spaceship *Pioneer 10.*

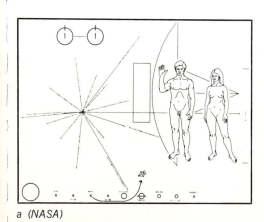

a (NASA)

b (West Los Angeles Times)

Figure 2-2

c (West Los Angeles Times)

A single idea, in writing as in the visual arts, can be developed in a seemingly infinite number of ways. The one you choose and with which you can be most successful is the one that reflects your strongest feelings—in other words, you.

Sentences are a fusion of a group of ideas that may be developed individually in subsequent sentences. The more ideas a sentence contains, the greater the possibilities of development. In the sentence below, we have italicized three areas that have been selected for further elaboration. Note the different direction that each elaboration takes.

Sentence:

Last Sunday I went on my *first sailboat ride,* and, I must confess, sailing could easily *become my favorite sport.*

Development:

LAST SUNDAY	FIRST SAILBOAT RIDE	BECOME MY FAVORITE SPORT
We began early, about 6 A.M., and planned to sail all day.	I had never known anyone with a boat before, and so I was never given the chance to sail one.	I had often seen sailboats in the Newport marina—a special breed among all the boats.
↓	↓	↓
Soon after arriving at the marina, we all were given specific things to do.	The invitation to do so came from a group of new friends.	Perhaps they were special because the people in them always seemed casual and fun loving.
↓	↓	↓
Some of us helped put up the sail while others loaded the boat with food and blankets.	I met them at a party given by an acquaintance of mine at Newport Beach.	Leaving the marina on my first sailboat ride that morning, I had much the same feeling I had observed in others.
↓	↓	↓
The day was exceptionally windy, which added to the excitement.	During dinner the group mentioned that they were going sailing and asked if anyone would like to come along.	As we entered the main body of water, a surge of excitement overcame me, and I knew this was *my* sport.
↓	↓	↓
etc.	etc.	etc.

EXERCISE

This exercise is divided into two parts: an individual effort and a group effort. Its intent is to show that the possible developments of a sentence greatly vary.

1. Individual assignment. On a separate piece of paper write a sentence which could be the first sentence of a story. Now develop the story with six more sentences.
2. Group assignment. After getting into a group of five or more, do the following:
   a. Copy the first sentence that you wrote for the individual assignment on a separate piece of paper.
   b. Pass it to the person on your left.
   c. The person on the left will add another sentence and pass it on to the person on his left who will do the same, etc.
   d. When the papers return to their original authors, they should be completed with a final sentence.
   e. There should be five or more simultaneously completed stories.
   f. Each person will read the story he began to the group and then read the story he himself wrote. The differences in their development should be noted.

OPTIONAL EXERCISE

Choose one of the drawings (Figure 2-2a, 2-2b, or 2-2c) and on a separate piece of paper write a letter to extraterrestrial men that you think might accompany a spacecraft on its mission through space.

chapter 3

I AM CREATIVE: MAKING THINGS

BASIC TOOLS

We have seen that the desire for self-expression is something we all share. We need not be professional writers or artists for that. And once we decide to let it happen, we all have the ability as well: we all have things to say and stories to tell.

But alike though we may be in desire and aptitude, the specific stories we tell and the way we tell them are usually quite different from those of other people.

This individual difference has a great deal to do with the *creative process.*

What is the creative process? In the narrowest sense, it is the act of "making things." But nothing is made out of nothing. When a child is asked to make a single cube out of four square blocks, he must start with the four blocks themselves. And even a clever versifier like Ogden Nash, when composing

> Candy is dandy
> But liquor is quicker

must make use of six common words, certain possibilities of rhyme and sound peculiar only to the English language, and one of many conceivable observations on the way young ladies respond. Indeed, no artist—not even a Shakespeare or Michelangelo—has ever created anything except with the tools immediately at hand, including specific words or colors, specific artistic conventions, and specific things seen or heard or heard about.

All this is obvious enough. Less obvious is the fact that some acts of "making things" are truly creative while others may not be creative in the least. All dictionaries agree that creativity is characterized by *originality* of thought and execution. For instance, the construction of a cube out of four blocks is hardly a challenge to anyone (except, of course, to a small child, whose response may involve a high degree of originality). On the other hand, Nash's two lines are very original. When we weigh the number of choices originally open to him against the final perfection of his poem, we must judge his undertaking an act of true creativity. Similarly, consider the scrambled words "the," "off," "keep," and "grass" (Think of them as unconnected, floating in midair). In nine out of ten minds, these words will yield the sentence "Keep off the grass." But the student who writes "Keep off the grass" is not being creative, because he is not thinking with originality. Instead, he is bowing to an automatic formula, an already-created thing. However, the student who writes "Keep the grass off" *is* perhaps creating something. At any rate he is choosing to look upon these four words as a fresh opportunity to contemplate man and his immemorial dealings with grass. The same can be said for the student who comes up with "Keep the off grass" or "Grass off the keep" or even "Off the grass keep"—all of which, incidentally, make perfectly good sense in English.

A creative response, then, may be described as one that

> Rejects the automatic formula (the *cliché*)
> Looks at the materials afresh
> Struggles to make something new

Thus, an artist's thinking *about* his tools—his words, paints, conventions, and observations—is itself a tool as important as all the other tools combined. And since one's thoughts and feelings are (or should be) entirely one's own, we return to our original assertion that *individual differences have a great deal to do with the creative process.*

EXERCISE

Make a complete original sentence out of the following scrambled words: "detergent," "house," "girl," "car," "sleep," "frighten," "Coke," "bat," "Miami," and "fire."

Rules: You may add one or two extra words—but as few as you feel are absolutely necessary. You may also add such "structure words" as "the," "a," "she," "her," "on," "in," and "after," and you may change the tense of the verbs ("Sleep" may be "slept," or "is sleeping"). In addition, you may use certain words in a variety of ways. For instance, the word "fire" can be used to express an action ("He fired her"), a thing ("a big fire"), or a comment on another thing ("a fire hose"). What about "sleep" and "house"? Words are really very flexible!

Your sentence: _____

_____

_____

DISCUSSION: (1) Read your sentence aloud in your group. (2) Which of the sentences in your group seems the most creative—which uses the words most unexpectedly? (3) Which seems the most predictable, the nearest to a cliché? (4) What other conclusions can be drawn from this experiment?

One conclusion is probably most apparent of all: No two sentences are quite alike. The odds against it are enormous. Your creative decisions are almost always as individual as your fingerprints.

THE UNCONSCIOUS

The unconscious mind, that mysterious storehouse of dreams and fantasies and buried memories, is all-important in real thinking—which is always creative thinking. When you first looked at "detergent," "house," "girl," "car," "sleep," "frighten," "Coke," "bat," "Miami," and "fire," you probably had no idea of how to fit all these words together. Nevertheless, you struggled with the problem.

WORD PROBLEM

> Period of struggle →

After a while you may have felt that the struggle would come to nothing. Often one simply gives up at this point.

WORD PROBLEM

> Period of struggle → Giving up →

Then suddenly the answer came. You probably found your solution all at once—an idea for a sentence that would fuse all these words together sensibly and satisfyingly. It usually comes in a flash. Psychologists call it *insight*.

WORD PROBLEM   SOLUTION

> Period of struggle → Giving up → Insight →

Recently, one of our students, Jim Lawrence, helped us to make a closer analysis of this process. Jim told us that, while working out this same word problem, his flash of insight had consisted of "Bat . . . frightens girl . . . in car." Immediately he knew that this was his solution and that this would be the core of his sentence. All the other words would have to be placed in secondary positions.

But why this solution in the first place? What inner magnet abruptly pulled these stray filings out of that word heap and fixed them in precisely *this* pattern—"Bat frightens girl in car"? (Why not "Bat girl put out the fire with detergent"?) Had Jim ever been frightened by a bat—or a snake, rat, or spider—in a car or some other small enclosure? Perhaps it had happened so long ago that his conscious mind forgot. Or had he only dreamed about such an encounter? Psychoanalysts are quick to point out that such dreams usually signify other, more deeply buried emotional experiences. In any case, it is probably not important *why* the thought of a girl frightened by a bat came easily; the important thing is that it *did* come—that some potent picture within Jim's unconscious mind was eager to shape itself into consciousness by assuming the first guise that came to hand, the guise provided by the scrambled words he started with. And Jim was able to work out the problem without further hesitation.

Jim's experience is true for all of us. When our really basic decisions come, they come as if unbidden, in a flash of insight, and only *after* we have given up trying to force answers from our minds. And they come from the unconscious mind, whose very substance is our own most intimate hopes and joys and memories and fears.

What we normally call "thinking," the act of conscious reasoning, is really only "afterthought." For example, when Jim made his statement, "Bat frightens girl in car," he was aware that he was temporarily rejecting the other words, and he knew that to complete the puzzle he would have to place these other words in secondary roles. He allowed for this at the time, and later he consciously worked out the process. He finished his sentence by writing, "During the Miami fire a sleeping bat in the house girl's car frightened her so much she drank detergent instead of coke". Thus, with a few last-minute adjustments, his total act of thought was complete.

WORD PROBLEM	SOLUTION	SOLUTION COMPLETED

> Period of struggle → Giving up → Insight → Afterthought

EXERCISES

1. Try answering some questions from an intelligence test. Each time you find a solution, pause to recall your thought processes. Underline your answers.

    a. If ten boxes full of apples weigh 300 pounds and each box when empty weighs 3 pounds, how many pounds do all the apples weigh?
       (1) 30   (2) 270   (3) 297   (4) 300   (5) 303

    b. If the words OHIO, NOON, ROTOR, and OTTO were seen on a wall by looking in a mirror on an opposite wall, how many of them would appear exactly the same as if seen directly?
       (1) 1   (2) 2   (3) 3   (4) 4   (5) 0

    c. One number is wrong in this series: 1, 2, 4, 7, 11, 16, 22, 28. What should that number be?
       (1) 3   (2) 6   (3) 10   (4) 29   (5) 15

    d. If the words below were arranged to make a good sentence, with what letter would the second word of the sentence begin?
       same   means   small   little   the   as
       (1) s   (2) m   (3) l   (4) t   (5) a*

DISCUSSION: (1) Compare answers within your group. (2) Explain the basic insight that enabled you to find each one. (3) How much afterthought was involved?

*Arthur S. Otis, *Otis Quick-Scoring Mental Ability Tests*, Gamma Test: Form C. Copyright 1939 by Harcourt, Brace & World, Inc. Reprinted by permission of Harcourt Brace Jovanovich.

2.   Now try another word problem. Make a complete sentence out of "horse," "Holly-
       wood," "knife," "airplane," "dad," "laugh," "run," "boy," and "quickly." Again
       you may add a few extra words (very few), supply any necessary structure words,
       and change the tense of the verbs. And don't forget that some words can be used in
       more than one way. What about "laugh" and "knife" and "boy" and "run" in the
       present problem?

       Your sentence: _____

       _____

       _____

       DISCUSSION: (1) Read your sentence aloud in your group. (2) Which of the
sentences read seems the most creative? What is the basic idea of this sentence, the
focus of insight around which the other words are arranged?
       INTROSPECTION: What is the focus of your own sentence? Do you have any
inner clues to the source of this insight?

   One of the most direct approaches to the unconscious mind is the Rorschach ink-
blot test, used by psychologists the world over.

EXERCISES

Figure 3-1
(Gabriele Wunderlich)

1.   Look at the inkblot in Figure 3-1.

       DISCUSSION: What kind of picture do you see in this image? Compare your im-
pression with those of your group members.

Figure 3-2 *(Omikron)*

Figure 3-3 *(Omikron)*

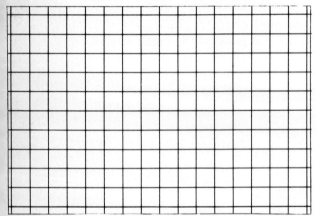

Figure 3-4

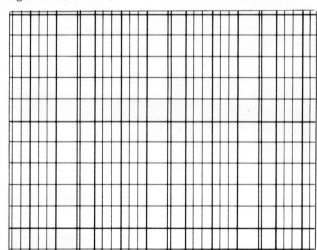

Figure 3-5

2.   A more active version of the inkblot test is the overlay game, a process of building pictures on odd and suggestive frameworks. For example, look at Figures 3-2 and 3-3. Taking off from these figures, superimpose some material of your own upon Figures 3-4 and 3-5. (Use either pen or pencil.)

DISCUSSION: Compare the pictures in your group. Decide which ones are the most original and the most interesting.

INTROSPECTION: Consider your own drawings. Do you have any inner clues to your own way of responding to this assignment?

Sometimes doodles and drawings can lead us to a direct grasp of our own deepest feelings about the world around us and thence to a set of ideas which can be put into words. Recently we asked some students, "Draw a picture of the world, of *everything*, as you see it and feel it." Figures 3-6, 3-7, and 3-8 are some of the pictures we received.

When asked for interpretations, each student was able to work up a clear verbal statement of his "view of the world." Student C explained his picture this way:

> The world is a tree—gnarled, perpetual, constantly assimilating everything. The portions of the tree are, of course, people. Some are solid, basic; others are frail, slender twigs; a few are blossoms, the lucky ones; the rest are leaves, an embellishment of many colors, supporting and adding to all the rest in different degrees. And all, after the fall, *die*.

Figure 3-6 Student A.

Figure 3-7 Student B.

Figure 3-8 Student C.

EXERCISES

On a blank sheet of paper, using pen or pencil, draw your own picture of the world. Try not to think it out too precisely, but rely on your feelings. Approach your picture as a process of discovery.

WRITING: After you have finished your drawing, examine it closely and then write down an interpretation.

DISCUSSION: (1) Examine all the pictures in your group. As each picture is shown, comment on your first impression of it. What kind of feelings does it express—what vibrations does it give off? (2) Read your interpretation of your own picture. As each interpretation is read, consider whether it really accounts for everything in the picture. If an interpretation does not seem to be complete, ask the writer for further details. (3) Do some of the interpretations seem to contradict the pictures they represent, as if the writer is trying to cover up his own gut feelings? Why are some pictures large and others small, filling only a small portion of the page? Why are some pictures simple and others very complicated? Why are some even and regular throughout and others quite sloppy? Why are some full of individual images, while others resort to lots of cut-and-dried symbols (such as a dollar sign or the Cross)? (4) Comment on the *ideas* expressed in each of the interpretations.

INTROSPECTION: (1) Silently consider this pictorial expression of your own personality and mental outlook, and compare yourself with others. (2) Did this drawing exercise help you to solidify some of your thoughts about the world—that is, have you achieved any new insights? Do these insights contradict any of your previously held notions? How can this contradiction be resolved?

CONFLICT

Any creative act is largely the resolution of a *conflict.* Our word and number games consisted of various possible solutions in conflict with one another and with our accompanying struggle to resolve them. Indeed, all games partake of conflict, and some come close to actual warfare. Consider hockey, football, poker, bridge, or Monopoly. The question, then, is why do we find warfare so engrossing? (Pacifists, those who deplore man's habit of solving his problems with real wars, have long asked this question in deadly earnest.) Robert Ardrey, in his book *African Genesis* (Atheneum Publishers, New York, 1961), suggests an answer when he asserts that we are all descended from a species of anthropoid called the "killer ape." This particular ape was unique among animals in that it habitually killed its own kind. If our wars and games are any indication, we certainly seem to share such personality traits. But there is a brighter side to the coin. Most of our games are only make-believe warfare. They are not meant to destroy us, but, on the contrary, to help us by releasing our hostilities while strengthening our bodies and sharpening our wits. Indeed, for all its evils, war itself is a great sharpener of wits. Surgical lasers and moon shots are only two of the by-products of recent wars. And it may well be that our inheritance of bellicose tendencies is the very root of all our wondrous intelligence and adaptability. It is even possible that our flair for conflict, expressing itself in acts of thought and works of art, may someday enable us to conquer the deadliest opponent of all—war itself.

So far we have been talking about games, problems, acts of thought, and works of art as if they were all alike. In certain basic essentials, *they are.* One who hates classical music may think of Mozart as a grim drudge who sadistically set out to punish himself and others with irritating noises. A dunce in physics may visualize Einstein's life as one long immersion in boredom. But in reality Mozart wrote all that music for only one reason: It was fun. Fun to pit a sad melody against a happy one and to let them clash with each other until one of them defeated the other or abandoned the other or harmoniously joined the other. And for Einstein physics was just as exciting. He began by trying to harmonize two great half-truths about the laws of motion (the mechanistic views of Newton and the conflicting explanations of Faraday and Maxwell in their field theory of electromagnetism), and after many years and countless partial solutions, he solved his problem so ably that today we have a unified theory of the dynamics of the whole universe. Nor did the delight in game conflicts that kept Mozart and Einstein active all their lives end with them. For two centuries music lovers have been reexperiencing the stirring interplay of opposites that is at the heart of every Mozart piece—his original delight in working out his musical problems. And for future generations of physicists, a step-by-step review of Einstein's relativity theory will continue to be a fascinating puzzle as well as a necessary training ground.

Now obviously there is a difference between a mere game and a scientific demonstration. But is the difference all that big? It is quite possible that Einstein's interest in motion began in childhood with the movements of tiddledywinks or marbles. And any infant who bangs on piano keys and enjoys the way one note sounds next to another may be a potential Mozart. And if he starts to experiment with crayons by making one line intersect another and by making one color darker than another, he may be playing Picasso's favorite childhood game. It has been said that a poet's indispensable gift is a simple delight in words themselves, in the way they look and sound and relate to one another. Emily Dickinson began by making up nonsense phrases, and a few years later her little word games evolved into a series of superb lyrics. Yet none of her poems ever lost the quality of play; no purpose, however serious, was allowed to eclipse the sheer joy of making words clash and mingle.

> Many a phrase has the English language,
> I have heard but one,
> Low as the laughter of the cricket,
> Loud, as the thunder's tongue.

We believe that the same thing holds true for all good works of the spirit and intellect. And so, to answer our own question, many a game may lead to nothing but pleasure, but no scientific demonstration is worth its salt that did not begin as a game. Our real motive force is always that love of conflict we call play.

Let us try to define *conflict*. When a student takes a creative writing course, he is often told, "A good story must have conflict." But does this mean that every good story has to read like "Gunsmoke"? Not at all. A husband and wife discussing their budget also exemplify conflict. So does a boy trying to get up the nerve to call a girl for a date: he is in conflict with his own timidity. Recently one of our students wrote a very effective short story about a girl who sees a porpoise. The girl is lying drowsily on the deck of a sailboat, vaguely enjoying the smell of the sea and the sound of the white sails billowing above her. Suddenly the porpoise shoots up in the distance, and this delights her. This story is quite complete, and it shows conflict perfectly. For in the fullest sense, conflict simply means that *one thing comes into contact with another thing and, in one way or another, grapples with it.* In our student's story it is porpoise against girl—the animal's sudden beauty playing upon her receptive state of mind.

But no story is complete without a *resolution* of the conflict, a feeling that the stronger of the two things wins out or at least permits a truce. And the point we are making is that "stronger" need not imply guns or fists; it may just as well mean the ability to persuade or captivate. In our student's story the girl is captivated by the porpoise. Its final resolution: She is deeply moved and will remember the experience.

Our word and number games are also instances of pure conflict. Within the mind that perceives them, each of the separate, unconnected words in "the," "off," "keep," "grass" is vying for some kind of relative dominance over all the others. One resolution of this conflict, as you may recall, was the sentence "Keep the grass off."

Now, in Figure 3-9, we will take a brief look at some of the other kinds of conflict that have occupied men's imaginations.

Our list could be expanded, but we trust that we have made our point. At the bottom of each of our mental occupations is the working out and resolving of some form of conflict.

One of the purest forms of conflict is the last item on our list, the play. A play is usually nothing more or less than a clash between people. Of course, if the clash is to mean anything we have to know what makes the people tick—their fears, their ambitions, and their abilities. Thus, every play begins by giving us information about its characters, but no more than is necessary to get the conflict under way. In a sense the playwright's task is an easy and natural one, for everybody is potentially in conflict with everybody else. (And remember, in our definition, conflict simply means any kind of close confrontation—even though Ardrey's "killer ape" may lurk somewhere in the background.) Whenever we see a boy and girl together, we involuntarily size up their relationship. Does she need him more than he needs her? Is she drawn to him for his money, his looks, his brains, or his personality? Would he like to shake her off and talk to that blonde across the room? Instinctively we imagine them into a conflict, size up its terms, and try to resolve it. And when

In a drawing:

{ Vertical lines
against diagonal lines
against horizontal lines

{ Cone against sphere

In a painting:

{ One color
against another color

{ Light against dark

In music:

{ Melody against counterpoint;
one key against another key;
sad theme against happy theme

{ Brass against strings

In a scientific or
philosophical treatise:

{ Species against individual;
general against specific;
cause against effect

In a play:

{ One character
against another character

{ Characters
against their environment

Figure 3-9. Conflicts.

we see one person alone, we usually evaluate that person's potential for conflict by relating him to our own feelings and past experiences. What would he do in this or that situation?

Figure 3-10. Barbara.
(Fisher–Omikron)

EXERCISES

1.   Look at the girl in Figure 3-10—we will call her Barbara. What do you think of Barbara? How would you describe her? Do you have any strong feelings about her personality or her character? How do you think she would relate to others? In other words, try to estimate her potential for conflict.

Write about her here: _____

_____

_____

_____

DISCUSSION: (1) Read your estimate of Barbara to the other members of your group. (2) Talk about any differences in viewpoint but be careful not to let others' opinions influence you too much. If you are clearly wrong about some obvious fact, admit it; otherwise, cling steadfastly to your own hunches. They are your most valuable tool in making human responses.

2.   Now look at Barbara and two other people, Jim and Mary (Figure 3-11a, b, and c). Make a private evaluation of Jim, then of Mary, just as you evaluated Barbara earlier. Now consider all three of them *together*. How might they relate to one another? Would they behave differently together than they would alone—especially Barbara, whom you have already sized up by herself?

a. Barbara

b. Jim. (A. Lopez–Omikron)

Figure 3-11.   c. Mary. (A. Lopez–Omikron)

WRITING: On a separate sheet of paper, write a little story about these three people. Using the past tense, tell who they were, how they were interrelated, and "what happened to them." Try not to introduce any other characters and be sure to leave no dangling "loose ends." That is, completely resolve the conflict you read into this relationship.

DISCUSSION: (1) Read your story aloud in your group. (2) Afterward comment on the different approaches used. (3) Was one story vastly more original than the rest? Why? (4) Did one very obvious approach appear in several stories? That was the cliché.

INTROSPECTION: Reconsider your own inner struggle for a solution to the problem of Barbara, Jim, and Mary. What flash of insight did you receive that enabled you to go ahead and write your story? Can you detect some kinship between these characters and people in your own life, including yourself? If your story was one of the least original in the group, you were probably not using material from your own life but were instead only echoing stories you have picked up from the movies or television. Next time, dig deeper into your own memories and experiences!

Again, drama is conflict in its purest form. Your story was not a play—that is, it was not made up exclusively of people talking in a fictitious present, but the conflicting relationships that made it work as a story were identical to the kind a playwright uses. Actually, there is a pure play at the bottom of all good stories and novels, however devious or long-winded they may be in the telling. And every nonfiction article that states a problem to be solved (which it must do if it is to hold interest) is making use of the same principle. For nothing is half so interesting all by itself as it is when set in opposition to something else. What is a horizontal line without a vertical? What is a sad theme without a happy one? What is a rule without its exceptions?

EXERCISE: READING, VIEWING, AND LISTENING

Taking each of the following selections in turn, consider the kind of conflict which it embodies. Remember that some conflicts are explicit while others are more subtle.

1.

It is hard to say what being a flier meant. I had friends I thought would last forever, and in combat, routinely, in the way it happened, I saved other pilots two or three times just as they did the same for me. There was a feeling for each other. We knew there was nobody like us, and for once in my life I thought I had found a home.

That home fell apart. I can even pick the day I remember best, and it did not happen in combat. Fighting an enemy plane was impersonal and had the nice moves of all impersonal contests; I never felt I had done anything but win a game. I flew a plane the way I used to box; for people who know the language I can say that I was a counter-puncher. As flight-time built up, I went stale, we all did, but it was the only time in my life when I was happy and didn't want to be somewhere else. Even the idea of being killed was not a problem for who wanted a life outside the Air Force? I never thought of what I would do afterward.

Sometimes on tactical missions we would lay fire bombs into Oriental villages. I did not like that particularly, but I would be busy with technique, and I would dive my plane and drop the jellied gasoline into my part of the pattern. I hardly thought of it any other way. From the air, a city in flames is not a bad sight.

One morning I came back from such a job and went into Officers' Mess for lunch. We were stationed at an airfield near Tokyo, and one of our Japanese K.P.'s, a fifteen-year-old boy, had just burned his arm in a kettle of spilled soup. Like most Orientals he was durable, and so he served the dishes with one hand, his burned arm held beneath him, while the sweat stood on his nose, and he bobbed his head in little shakes because he was disturbing our service. I could not take my eyes from the burn; it ran from the elbow to the shoulder, and the skin had turned to blisters. The K.P. began to get on my nerves. For the first time in years I started to think of my father and the hunchbacked boy and Sister Rose's lessons on my duty.

After lunch I took the Jap aside, and asked the cooks for tannic-acid ointment. There wasn't any in the kitchen, and so I told them to boil tea and put compresses to his arm. Suddenly, I realized that two hours ago I had been busy setting fire to a dozen people, or two dozen, or had it been a hundred?

No matter how I tried to chase the idea, I could never get rid of the Japanese boy with his arm and his smile. Nothing sudden happened to me, but over a time, the thing I felt about most of the fliers went false. I began to look at them in a new way, and I didn't know if I liked them. They were one breed and I was another; they were there and I was a fake. I was close to things I had forgotten, and it left me sick; I had a choice to make. My missions were finished, my service was over, and I had to decide if I wanted to sign for a career in the Air Force. Trying to make up my mind I got worse, I had a small breakdown, and spent a season in the hospital. I was not very sick, but it was a breakdown, and for seven weeks I lay in bed and felt very little. When I got up, I learned that I was to be given a medical discharge. It no longer mattered. . . .*

—Norman Mailer

2.
My mistress' eyes are nothing like the sun;
Coral is far more red than her lips' red:
If snow be white, why then her breasts are dun;
If hairs be wires, black wires grow on her head.
I have seen roses damasked, red and white,
But not such roses see I in her cheeks;
And in some perfumes is there more delight
Than in the breath that from my mistress reeks.
I love to hear her speak, yet well I know

*Norman Mailer, *The Deer Park*, G. P. Putnam Sons, New York, 1955. This excerpt is from pp. 44–45 of the Signet Edition.

That music hath a far more pleasing sound:
I grant I never saw a goddess go, —
My mistress, when she walks, treads on the ground:
    And yet, by heaven, I think my love as rare
    As any she belied by false compare.

—William Shakespeare

3.

A man said to the universe:
"Sir, I exist!"
"However," replied the universe,
"The fact has not created in me
A sense of obligation."

—Stephan Crane

4.

I wandered lonely as a cloud
That floats on high o'er vales and hills,
When all at once I saw a crowd,
A host of golden daffodils,
Beside the lake, beneath the trees,
Fluttering and dancing in the breeze.

Continuous as the stars that shine
And twinkle on the milky way,
They stretched in never-ending line
Along the margin of a bay;
Ten thousand saw I at a glance,
Tossing their heads in sprightly dance.

The waves beside them danced, but they
Outdid the sparkling waves in glee—
A poet could not but be gay
In such a jocund company.
I gazed—and gazed—but little thought
What wealth the show to me had brought:

For oft when on my couch I lie
In vacant or in pensive mood,
They flash upon that inward eye
Which is the bliss of solitude,
And then my heart with pleasure fills,
And dances with the daffodils.

—William Wordsworth

5.

Excess of sorrow laughs. Excess of joy weeps.

The fox provides for himself, but God provides for the lion.

Think in the morning. Act in the noon. Eat in the evening. Sleep in the night.

The tigers of wrath are wiser than the horses of instruction.

The crow wished everything was black, the owl that everything was white.

Sooner murder an infant in its cradle than nurse unacted desires.

The eagle never lost so much time as when he submitted to learn of the crow.

What is now proved was once only imagined.

—William Blake

6.

Figure 3-12. Pablo Picasso, *Guernica,* oil on canvas (11 ft 5½ in. x 25 ft 5¾ in.), 1937 (May–early June). On extended loan to the Museum of Modern Art, New York, from the artist.

7.

If a phonograph or tape recorder is available, play a few songs or brief orchestral movements and discuss the kinds of conflict inherent in each—whether of theme, rhythm, instrumentation, "musical story," or all of these together. Try for variety, striking a balance between, for example, rock, folk, and classical.

chapter 4

I AM CREATIVE: THE THING MADE

ONENESS

Although it is important to understand the process of making things, our investigation cannot end there. Whenever a creative act may be said to have occurred, there is always something to point to—the created thing. The psychologist Carl R. Rogers puts it this way: "Though my fantasies may be extremely novel, they cannot usefully be defined as creative unless they eventuate in some observable product—unless they are symbolized in words, or written in a poem, or translated into a work of art, or fashioned into an invention."

However, not all poems or works of art or invention are created equal. In a sense, some are more *created* than others. What we are saying, then, is that Roger's "observable product" must meet certain standards before it can be called the product of a truly creative act.

The most basic standard is *oneness*. The thing made must be *one thing*. Look at Figures 4-1 and 4-2. Obviously the first picture qualifies as one thing: a cat sitting. But what about the second? It looks as if someone accidentally stuck the halves of two different photographs onto the same page. It cannot rightly be called a picture at all.

Figure 4-1 *(Colette Barati–Omikron)*

Figure 4-2 *(Colette Barati–Omikron)*

Figure 4-3 *(Colette Barati–Omikron)*

Figure 4-4. Albrecht Durer, *Junger Feldhase (Hare)*. Fonds Albertine, Vienna.

So far we have been using the word "oneness" to mean a choice of subject matter. Is our picture going to show a garbage can or a city skyline? Yet few pictures are so indecisive that they lack this basic surface oneness. Even the most amateurish of snapshots is usually an attempt, however inept, to capture some one person or thing.

More properly used, "oneness" means something that happens within an already limited subject area. Compare Figures 4-3 and 4-4. The photo in Figure 4-3 shows us somebody's cat, but the obvious lack of care for lighting and composition make the cat seem as incidental as all the objects cluttered around it. It is as if we see the cat for a mere second with the most casual and mindless of glances. But the painting in Figure 4-4 (Dürer's *Hare*) has the kind of *inner* oneness we are talking about. Not only does it exclude anything that would distract us from its subject, the hare, but its loving concentration on every detail makes us know this hare more intimately than most any animal we are likely to see in real life. Indeed, this painting is so well executed that many people feel that it is really a kind of meditation on the life force as manifested in one of nature's humblest creatures. Still, there is no question that is *about* a hare.

A picture may have a lot more detail than Dürer's *Hare* and still have total oneness. An example is El Greco's masterful *View of Toledo* (Figure 4-5). Note that every detail in this painting blends with every other, and they all fuse together into a single powerful image. They all make one thing.

Figure 4-5. El Greco (Domenicos Theotocopoulos), Spanish, 1541–1614, *View of Toledo,* oil on canvas (47¾ in.x 42¾ in.). The Metropolitan Museum of Art, New York. Bequest of Mrs. H. O. Havermeyer, 1929. The H. O. Havermeyer Collection.

Figure 4-6

Figure 4-7

Figure 4-8 *(Gabriele Wunderlich)*

EXERCISES

1.   Look at Figures 4-6, 4-7, and 4-8.

DISCUSSION: (1) Which of the three do you think has the most oneness? That is, which one seems most concentrated, most emphatically *about* one thing, and most likely to stick in your memory? (2) Which picture has the least oneness?

2.   Consider these two short paragraphs.

a

It was a depressing afternoon. I couldn't go out because my car's brakes were shot. I couldn't eat because the refrigerator was empty. I couldn't finish my term paper because my sister had taken my typewriter to her girl friend's house. On top of all that, my fiancée called me up to tell me she was getting married to my best friend.

b

A used car can be a source of grief. My friend Tom recently bought an old Studebaker. He has had quite a long history of car troubles. Perhaps he inherited that tendency from his father, a onetime ambassador to Holland, where people are more accustomed to bicycles, which have the virtue of giving your body exercise and not adding to air pollution.

DISCUSSION: Which of these two paragraphs has the most oneness? Compare your opinion with those of your group members.

WRITING: On a separate sheet of paper, write a brief paragraph—about the length of those above. Give it the utmost oneness: make every detail point to one idea with all the concentration you can bring to bear. *State this main idea in your very first sentence (This is the topic sentence).* Examples: It was a depressing afternoon. A used car can be a source of grief. Girls (or boys) can be very unreasonable.

DISCUSSION: (1) When you have finished your paragraph, read it aloud in your group. (2) Which paragraph has the most oneness? (3) Do some of them drift noticeably from their topic idea? If so, how and where?

THE IMAGE

The cat picture in the last section projected a weak image. *Hare* and *View of Toledo* conveyed very strong images. A strong image may be defined as one that contains *enough* detail (not too much, not too little), all sufficiently harmonized to create a clear, concentrated, single effect. That is, it has inner oneness. Works of art—pictures, stories, plays, songs, and sculptures—are works of art only insofar as they succeed in transmitting strong images.

As every politician knows, people project images just as pictures do. Let us compare good and bad images in these human terms.

Al (Figure 4-9) projects a bad image. He lacks oneness because he dislikes himself; he is at war with himself. His future plans are weakened because he is always dwelling on his past failures. His thoughts clash with his actions. His words seem phony because he cannot say what he means. His speech is oddly affected, and he rambles. His clothes are both pretentious and carelessly selected. Because he dislikes himself, others dislike him. In other words, since his own unlikability is his surest reality, he achieves security by making others share it, subtly and often unconsciously turning their friendly overtures into the distaste he understands. And when he wants something, he is so sure that people will deny him that his very request is secretly designed to ensure rejection.

Bill (Figure 4-10) projects a good image. He has oneness because he likes himself in the best sense; that is, he is at peace with himself—his past is in harmony with his present, his thoughts with his actions, his feelings with his appearance, his speech and dress and manner with his age and intelligence, and his idea of himself with reality. Because he knows what he wants, he is able to ask for it naturally, and others usually find it just as easy and natural to respond. People like Bill because he likes himself.

So a good image, whether in man or art, is one that knows what it is and what it wants and asks its due as directly as possible.

Figure 4-9. Al. (E. Baitel–Omikron)

Figure 4-10. Bill. (A. Lopez–Omikron)

Figure 4-11 *(Harlan Hoffman)*

Figure 4-12 *(A. Lopez–Omikron)*

EXERCISE

Look at the two people shown in Figures 4-11 and 4-12.

Which of them has the most attractive image? That is, which seems the most *at one* with herself?

DISCUSSION: Compare your opinion (and your reasons for it) with the opinions of your group members.

INTROSPECTION: Look into yourself and consider whether your own thoughts and wishes and capabilities are in harmony with one another and whether you are able to project these things to others in such a way that they regard you as you wish to be regarded. If you feel that the "real you" is not getting across to people as a strong, effective image, ask yourself why. Does one part of you contradict another? Do you like the clothes you are wearing—do they really express *you?* Does your habitual way of speaking enable you to say the things you really want to say?

Now look around at some of your classmates and silently evaluate the effectiveness of the image each of these persons projects. What overall impressions do you receive? Also consider such guidelines as clothing, speech, posture, and body language.

Figure 4-14

Figure 4-15

Figure 4-16

Figure 4-13. Antonio Pollaiuolo, *Saint Sebastian.* Courtesy of
The National Gallery, Washington, D.C.

THE ALL-AT-ONCE IMAGE VERSUS THE CUMULATIVE IMAGE

By using the word "image," we have been talking in visual terms. And ordinarily a
visual image is something we experience all at once—like the face on a coin, the
design on a dish, or the content of a picture. Even the most complicated painting will
usually reveal itself in a moment as a complete image (Figure 4-13). It is only after
we have grasped this complete image that we may be tempted to examine its details,
the subtle interplay of its lines and shapes and tones (Figures 4-14, 4-15, and 4-16).
But if the picture is well made, these details only thrust themselves (and us) back
into the dominant center of the composition, the *all-at-once* image (Figure 4-13).

The best way to grasp this is to look at a picture that is *not* well made, one that lacks balance and oneness: for example, Figure 4-17. When we look at this painting, we find our attention shunted from side to side. Our search for a satisfying image is frustrated. We feel the kind of anxiety we might feel in a house without a living room or in the company of an indecisive person like Al.

Fortunately, paintings like this one rarely reach the art books or museums; they usually end up in somebody's attic or trash can. However, a goodly share of bad pictures are thrust upon us in the form of amateur snapshots, and you can see why those albums and slide collections have often bored you silly. Next time it happens, feast your eyes on Figure 4-18 for an antidote. And remember, a good picture presents a solid image *all at once.*

Now consider the art forms that move: songs, symphonies, plays, poems, stories, novels, and films. Moving forms like these do not reveal themselves all at once. They flow along, one thing happening after another. Yet a critic discussing a poem or story will often speak of the "image" it creates, as if these forms were capable of producing the kind of all-at-once revelation we find in a picture.

In a certain sense moving art forms do present a solid image. Although one thing happens after another in a piece of music or writing, the last thing does not simply

Figure 4-17. Cornelius van Poelenburgh, *The Annunciation.* Gemäldegalerie, Kunsthistorisches Museum, Vienna.

Figure 4-18. Rembrandt Harmensz van Rijn, 1606–1669, *Christ Preaching,* etching. The Metropolitan Museum of Art. Bequest of Mrs. H. O. Havermeyer, 1929.

die away; the final image is retained in our minds and is added onto preceding things. What happens here may be compared to the psychological phenomenon of the *afterimage,* by means of which we continue to "see" a shape or color after we have looked away from it. And finally, if the composition is well begun (in music with a dominant key, in fiction with a provocative scene, and in nonfiction with a clearly stated topic) and if each of the parts is successively clear, all the parts will fall into place as effectively as the colors on a canvas and yield the same kind of solid image.

It is only when the development of the moving form strays from the mood-setting key, the involving first scene, or the gripping premise that we feel the absence of a final cumulative image and experience the kind of anxiety that we get from a bad picture. Moreover, if the development is wayward, the parts themselves will seem to slip out of their groove and will be forgotten. The same thing can happen, whether or not the development seems consistent with the beginning, if the successive parts of the song or poem or story constitute weak and forgettable images.

Let us simplify this rather complex idea. Think of a pictorial image as a girl standing before you to be interviewed (Figure 4-19). Now think of a nonpictorial (or story) image as the same girl first seen dimly on the opposite bank of a stream (Figure 4-20). In order to appear before you, she must cross a bridge, inch by inch, step by step. With each successive step the girl comes closer (Figure 4-21). When the entire expanse of the bridge has been put behind her, the girl will step onto your side of the stream and come before you, ready to be interviewed, as solid in your consciousness as the image in the picture (Figure 4-22).

Figure 4-19

Figure 4-20

We have described the successive parts of a musical or verbal composition (the "steps" across our "bridge") as *images*. We have spoken of the entire composition as something designed to produce a single image (the girl who finally appears). What we have, then, is a series of small image units adding up to a single *cumulative image*.

Consider "The Eagle," by Tennyson:

He clasps the crag with hookèd hands;	(1)
Close to the sun in lonely lands,	(2)
Ring'd with the azure world he stands.	(3)
The wrinkled sea beneath him crawls;	(4)
He watches from his mountain walls;	(5)
And like a thunderbolt he falls.	(6)

Note the succession of images: (1) *The eagle clasps the crag.* (2) *He is close to the sun in lonely terrain.* (3) *He is surrounded by the blue sky.* These three separate images (the first stanza) give us a cumulative image of the eagle and tell us where he is and what he is doing. The second stanza builds another image: (4) *He sees the ocean beneath him.* (5) *He watches.* (6) *Then he falls like a thunderbolt.* Note that the second stanza parallels the first. Yet it also does more: It builds upon and absorbs the first stanza

ure 4-21

Figure 4-22

so that it is really an accumulation of cumulative images. And line 6, when it comes, is both the poem's main image, its point, and a final absorption of all that precedes it. What we are meant to carry away with us is the image of the eagle dropping, and we do. Without the bridge of images leading up to it, the eagle's fall would mean little and would soon be forgotten.

To further drive home our point, here is a direct equation of a picture with a descriptive paragraph.

In a picture, the image is complete all at once (Figure 4-23).

In writing, an image is built up with a series of details, one following the other.

Topic Sentence (presents a general outline and builds an expectation of the complete image to be built up).   Glenn was a smooth operator (Figure 4-24).

First Supporting Detail (Figure 4-25).   His eyes twinkled with confidence, and his smirky little grin made you want to watch your girl friend when he came around.

Second Supporting Detail (Figure 4-26).   His luxuriant blond hair was styled like a movie star's with roguish little tufts curling over his ears and down the nape of his neck.

Third Supporting Detail (Figure 4-27).   His fashionable blazer fit him with glovelike snugness, and his necktie was a winning compromise between mod boldness and conservative good taste.

Note, however, that a descriptive paragraph like this one can include additional details which a picture can only suggest. For example:

Fourth Supporting Detail.   His scent was a bit too much—a heady blend of Old Spice Pre-Electric and English Leather after-shave, but he rather doubted that women would hold that against him.

Fifth Supporting Detail.   Glenn never denied his obvious fascination for the opposite sex, and he attributed his success with women mainly to his lifelong study of karate. "The feeling they get that this guy's a deadly weapon walking around— it's worth more than all the con artistry in the world." Still, he had plenty of con to spare.

Now your image is complete.

EXERCISES

WRITING: Using our "smooth operator" as a model, develop a similar word portrait into an effective cumulative image. Start by forming a complete mental picture of the person you are describing, then allow various portions of this picture to come forth as a series of clear supporting details, each establishing a vivid image in its turn.

Figure 4-23

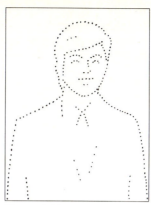

Figure 4-24

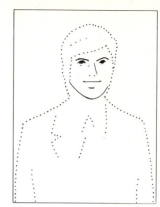

Figure 4-25

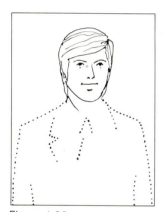

Figure 4-26

Figure 4-27

When you have exhausted the resources of your mental *picture*, add some of the things pictures can only suggest as we did in our fourth and fifth supporting details.

Topic sentence (an expectation of the entire image to come): _____

_____

_____

First supporting detail: _____

_____

_____

Second supporting detail: _____

Third supporting detail: _____

_____

_____

Fourth supporting detail: _____

_____

_____

Fifth supporting detail: _____

_____

_____

Sixth supporting detail: _____

_____

_____

DISCUSSION: Read your paragraph to your group. As each of the other paragraphs is read, evaluate the successive images. Are they vivid and effective in their
turn? Do they follow one another clearly and logically? Do they all add up to a satisfying cumulative image?

MEDITATING: (1) Play a few songs on your class phonograph or tape recorder.
Consider the separate notes and phrases — how each strikes you (can you see a color?)
or makes you feel or picture something. What about the whole song? What total image
do you finally formulate? What is the song's final effect? *Discuss at some length.* (2) Reread the passage from Norman Mailer beginning on page 70 in Chapter 3. Examine its
component images and evaluate it as a single cumulative image. *Discuss.* (3) Follow
the same procedure with the poems on pages 71–73. *Discuss.* (4) Finally, review Figure
3-12 as a completely integrated visual image. How and why do its lines and shapes
colors blend and mesh together? *Discuss.*

chapter 5

I AM A CAMERA: THE SENTENCE

THE SENTENCE IMAGE

Your reader will not be able to receive the complex total image we discussed in Chapter 4 unless this total image is carefully built up from a series of smaller and simpler images. Each image must be clearly effective in its turn, for a reader is capable of grasping only one thing at a time. In writing, therefore, your first step is to consider the most basic image unit.

At first glance the smallest image unit would appear to be the word. However, as we saw in our discussion of the creative process, words have a way of losing themselves in one another. For example, the words "boy," "sleep," "house," and "night" readily combine themselves into "The house boy sleeps all night" or "The boy sleeps in the house at night." We are irresistibly tempted to juggle words around until they land in sentences, and ordinarily we are no more aware of these individual words than of the molecular components of a drop of water.

So the first perceivable image unit in writing is the *sentence*.

Just what is a sentence? According to linguistics scholars it began as the cry. A prehistoric hunter, spear at the ready, might have cried out, "Moose!" or sounds to that effect. From the angle of his spear, the movement of his eyes, or the tone of his voice, his nearest companions could determine the location and perhaps even the size and sex of the moose. A modern hunter in similar circumstances would probably have to say, "We can get a bead on a bull moose as soon as he passes under the tree to the right of that big rock." Now the caveman's cry would be lost on a companion unfamiliar with his special idiosyncrasies, with the surrounding countryside, and with hunting as a regular mode of living. But the modern hunter need not worry: He can communicate with any greenhorn because he is confident of his ability to reduce the whole situation to fixed word symbols and manipulate them with precision. Yet, given their particular circumstances, both the caveman and the modern hunter would be capable of transmitting effective images of a moose.

Simply by saying that the sentence—and its ancestor, the cry—is a means of presenting an image, we are again comparing it to a picture, for a picture's only reason for existence is the image that constitutes it. Although we have already touched on the picturelike qualities of the sentence, we will develop the comparison further.

First, any good picture has overall *oneness*. Even if it includes lots of different things, these things must somehow all tie together as one thing, one subject. In the same way, even a loosely written sentence starts by being roughly about one thing:

Figure 5-1. Main Street.

On Main Street you can see restaurants, hotels, shops, traffic, glaring neon signs, and lots of other things (Figure 5-1).

Second, an *effective* picture has a more concentrated, *inner* oneness. Even if it seems to include many things, only one of these things clearly stands out (is what the picture is *about*), and all the others merely help to provide a setting or to give

←— Focal plane

Figure 5-2 *(Harlan Hoffman)*

the picture emphasis. We call this one thing the "center of interest." In a photograph it is the "focal plane" (Figure 5-2). A simple camera lens can focus on only one plane at a time, and objects in front of and behind the plane focused upon will appear in varying degrees of unsharpness or, as we say, "out of focus."

Similarly, when we read a sentence we are usually focusing on one center of interest, one actor-action relationship at a time. Everything surrounding this focal center is only extra comment. For example:

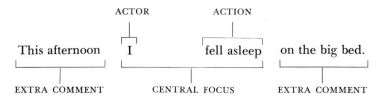

In a grammar textbook the "actor" of a sentence is called the "subject," and the "action" is called the "verb."

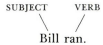

Also, a sentence is customarily divided into *subject* and *predicate.* Subject again means "actor," but predicate includes, in addition to the verb (simple action), any extra comment on its nature or direction (developed action).

This kind of analytical separation of parts (actor-action, subject-verb, and subject-predicate) can be useful. It helps us to pinpoint trouble spots when they occur in our reading or writing. But an approach to the sentence that is *only* analytical can be misleading, because no sentence is ever written or spoken for the sake of analysis. Analysis, after all, is something done in a cool, detached state of mind *after* reading has occurred. But it is not reading, and a sentence is written only to be read—to be perceived in flight.

The sentence, like any other form of moving art (a song, a poem, or a play), exists mainly to create the kind of single image that we find in a picture. For example, when we look at Figure 5-3, we are not conscious of any separation of the boy and his running. They are fused together as a single image. In the same way, when we first read "The boy runs," we are scarcely more aware of the separation. Once the sen-

Figure 5-3

tence passes into our minds, we perceive something like "boyruns." The subject and verb merge into a single image. So the analysis into subject and verb is at most rather temporary. It does not exist in the mind of the writer, nor in the mind of the reader; it exists only on paper as a sort of halfway station between two points.

EXERCISE

Look at Figures 5-4, 5-5, 5-6, and 5-7. What is the central focus of each picture? Write it down in the subject-verb pattern, adding some extra comment (EC) around it. Try to make each image come through as clearly in your sentence as it does in the picture. Example:

Figure 5-4:

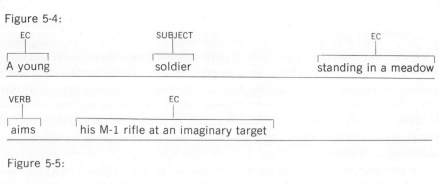

Figure 5-5:

Figure 5-6:

_____

_____

_____

Figure 5-7:

_____

_____

_____

DISCUSSION: (1) Read your sentences aloud in your group. (2) As each sentence is read, try to grasp it in your mind as an image. How clear is the picture it conveys? Is there a vivid central focus (like "a soldier aims")? (3) Does the extra comment help to fill out the picture, or does it distract you? Why? (4) Decide which one of the sentences read is the most effective. Consider why.

Figure 5-4

Figure 5-5

Figure 5-6 *(Omikron)*

Figure 5-7

SENTENCE VARIETIES

Lest we stand accused of oversimplification, we will pause briefly to consider some of the ways that sentences vary in scope and length and method of construction.

Roughly speaking, sentences fall into five basic patterns, as follows:

1. *Some sentences are single sentences.* The sentence above is an example of a single sentence. It has one subject ("sentences") and one verb ("are"). Reread it.

EXERCISE

Write one single sentence in the space that follows. Make it as funny or interesting as you can. _____

_____

DISCUSSION: (1) Read your sentence to your group. (2) Did everybody follow the prescribed pattern?

2. *When leaning sentences occur.* The preceding is an example of a leaning sentence. It has a subject (sentences) and a verb (occur), but because it starts with "when," *it cannot stand by itself*; it must *lean* for support against another sentence, like this: "When leaning sentences occur, they must find support." (Other words that make sentences lean are "if," "since," "because," "although," "before," "after," "until," and so on.)

EXERCISE

Write one leaning sentence here. _____

_____ *Read aloud and discuss.*

3. *When a leaning sentence is attached to a single sentence, the result is a sentence plus.* The preceding is an example of a sentence plus. Reread it.

EXERCISE

Write one sentence plus here. _____

_____

_____ *Read aloud and discuss.*

4.   *A single sentence is fine, but a double sentence has its virtues.* The preceding is
     an example of a double sentence. It has two subject-verb combinations (sen-
     tence . . . is and sentence . . . has). Reread it.

   EXERCISE

Write one double sentence here. _____

_____

_____

_____ *Read aloud and discuss.*

5.   *When a leaning sentence is attached to a double sentence, the result is a double
     sentence plus, and this is an example.* Indeed it is an example of a double sentence
     plus. Reread it.

   EXERCISE

Write one double sentence plus here. _____

_____

_____

_____

_____ *Read aloud and discuss.*

   Obviously a great many more combinations of these basic patterns are possible.
For instance, any single sentence can have more than one subject ("The *boys* and
girls were pleased") or more than one verb ("He *woke up* and *went* to the kitchen").
Also, a second leaning sentence can be added to an existing sentence plus ("*When*
he came in I left *because* I can't stand him") to make a sentence plus two, and that
construction can in turn be hooked onto a triple sentence plus to make a forbidding-
ly long quadruple sentence plus three, and so forth. As you can see, our labeling
has become rather cumbersome by now, but we trust that we have made our point.
   In addition to the type of construction it uses, a sentence can be greatly expanded
by *modifiers*—those "extra-comment" expressions that add color and qualification
and direction. Take, for example, the single sentence "George lay down." With a
few modifiers this sentence can be transformed into "*Feeling utterly exausted, my*

brother George *gratefully* lay down *on the dusty air mattress.*" (The modifiers are the words in italics.)

The reader who wishes a comprehensive review of all the intricacies of sentence structure, including a detailed discussion of the use of modifiers, is urged to turn immediately to Chapter 9.

THE SNAPSHOT

Think of the sentence as a snapshot.

Imagine that you have just checked into a hotel room in a small country town. You sit down at a desk and start to write a postcard to your family. As you prepare your brief message, you decide to say something about the hick-town atmosphere that surrounds you. A one-sentence description of your view from the hotel window will be enough. You cast a casual eye out of the window, and you see:

> A row of houses and buildings . . . a hotel . . . a brick grocery store be-
> side it . . . an old car parked in the driveway of a house with a shingle
> roof . . . which is next to a dry-cleaning shop . . . which adjoins a small
> boxy house with a TV antenna on top . . . next to an old house with a
> picket fence . . . and then back to the hotel . . . which adjoins a house with
> a large screened porch . . . standing next to a vacant lot containing one
> lone tree . . . which in turn adjoins a little cafe with a sign on top of it. . . .

Obviously your casual eye sees too much all at once. Thus, it *sees* practically nothing—nothing, that is, that can be reduced to a single image. Consequently, your first step as a writer is to *see less*. You must force your "mind's eye" to look through the viewfinder of an imaginary camera.

You do just that, but the result is frustrating. Your viewfinder picks up the shin-gle-roofed house with the car in its driveway, but it excludes too many other things. Your camera's frame is awfully narrow.

Then, after a moment of disappointment, you notice a tall stone chimney rising out of the shingle roof, and you decide that the house and car together add up to a satisfying image all their own (Figure 5-8):

> WORD PICTURE
> An antique car is parked in the driveway of an old house with a shingle
> roof and a tall stone chimney.

You are about to snap our picture, and then you pause. You are taken by the antique car. You notice that it is a Model T, beautifully restored, with a yellow can-vas top. In an attempt to give it more emphasis, you move your camera to the left,

Figure 5-8 *(Nancy Enkoji)*

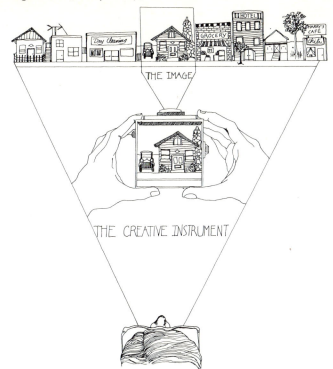

THE IMAGE

THE CREATIVE INSTRUMENT

THE CASUAL EYE

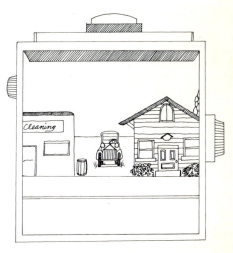

Figure 5-9 *(Nancy Enkoji)*

cutting some of the house out of your viewfinder while bringing the car closer to the center (Figure 5-9):

WORD PICTURE
Standing in the driveway of an old red-roofed house is a beautifully re-stored Model T Ford with a bright new canvas top.

Again you are about to snap your picture, but suddenly your attention shifts to the other buildings on the street. You observe that the roof of the brick grocery store is trimmed with ironwork, and you warm to the old hotel and the pretty elm tree in the vacant lot and the cafe on the corner. Somehow your picture wouldn't be right without these things. You have misgivings.

At last you decide to shoot the whole street after all. But in order to do so you must move back a great distance. You try it, and when you have finally squeezed everything into your viewfinder, you find that it all seems very distant. True, you have produced an interesting skyline (and a pleasing image), but only at the expense of all those details which have struck your fancy (Figure 5-10):

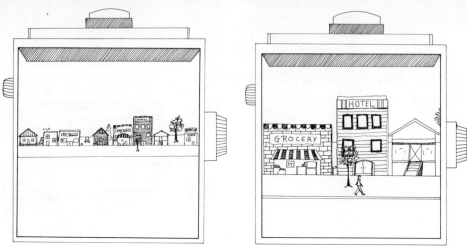

Figure 5-10 *(Nancy Enkoji)*   Figure 5-11 *(Nancy Enkoji)*

WORD PICTURE
Across a wide avenue, a row of variously shaped buildings rests beneath
a vast expanse of sky.

In despair you say to yourself, "If I were writing a paragraph, I could do it like a
movie: first, shoot the whole skyline, then cut to a middle distance, and then cut to
closeups of the best-looking buildings." But you are not writing a paragraph; you are
writing only one sentence, and all you really need is a simple but representative
snapshot. So you step forward once more, and soon the frame of your picture shrinks
to include only the vacant lot and the small cafe. Now you notice that the cafe is
called "Harry's" and serves chili. A good image might include the elm tree linked
to Harry's Cafe, but is it what you want? You start moving your camera around,
shifting your central emphasis from Harry's to the tree, to the next house, and beyond. As you do this, all the different possibilities are clashing with one another and
with your own purpose, and the creative process is in full swing.

Finally your pangs of selection are resolved. You decide to photograph the old
hotel (you see it is clapboard) flanked by the brick grocery with the ironwork and the
house with the screened porch. There are several good reasons for this arrangement.
First, the variety of styles and materials and textures that it offers seems to catch
the small-town mood you are after. Second, it includes a small tree growing out of
a crack in the sidewalk—a good substitute for the elm tree you cannot use. Third,
you see a typical old farmer walking up the street; you know you can catch him as
he passes, and that clinches it. Finally, the most important *why* of all, this arrangement simply "feels right" to you—an essential ingredient in any creative decision.

You take your picture, and the message on your postcard is complete (Figure
5-11):

WORD PICTURE

As I look out my window, I see an old clapboard hotel squeezed in between a brick grocery store with an iron roof and ancient house with a screened porch; a farmer is passing—stepping around a tree growing out of the sidewalk.

USING YOUR CAMERA

Just as a real camera forces you to render unbounded, three-dimensional space on a framed-in, two-dimensional surface, your imaginary camera makes you view the chaos of your thoughts and perceptions with a sympathetic insight into your reader's very limited moment-to-moment perceptions. But remember: Any camera is essentially no more than an eye without a brain. It is up to you to supply the brain.

For an idea of how to do this, look at the five main considerations which led to the final "snapshot" in the last section:

1. *Purpose* of the communication (sentence for a postcard)
2. *Observation* and *assessment* of details (the casual eye)
3. The establishment of a *frame* and *center of interest* (what to include)
4. The *relationship* of one thing to another (what to stress)
5. The *personal touch* (It feels right.)

Now once again:

1. *Purpose* of the communication. You undoubtedly have a purpose, or you would not bother to write at all. It is the specific nature of your purpose that makes all the difference.

EXERCISE

WRITING: Think of some very terrible or scandalous incident you recently witnessed or heard about or even just imagined. Using the most neutral, unbiased language possible (as if you were writing a straight news story), explain the crux of this incident in *one sentence.*

Straight news-story version: _____

_____

_____

Now describe the same incident as though you intended your one sentence to be included in the following:

A Christmas note to an elderly maiden aunt: _____

_____

_____

A complaint to the police: _____

_____

_____

A comedian's script: _____

_____

_____

A letter to a close friend: _____

_____

_____

DISCUSSION: Read your five sentences to the group. As others are read, compare the varying approaches used. Talk about them and note how differences in purpose seem to change the very "facts" of an incident.

2. *Observation* and *assessment* of details. The capacity of your camera's viewfinder is limited, so you must begin by surveying your field of choice.

EXERCISE

Look closely at Figure 5-12. Then, on a separate sheet of paper, make a careful list of its contents. Describe each item briefly but accurately, with an eye for significant details.

DISCUSSION: (1) Read your list to the group and compare it with other lists. (2) Consider any variations among the items noted. Why are some lists fuller than others? Why are certain details included in one list and omitted in another? (3) Concentrate on something in the picture that you failed to identify. Did you really not see it, or did you see it yet find it so hard to label that you let it pass? In other words, was the failure one of observation or of vocabulary? Discuss possible methods of improvement.

3. *Frame* and *center of interest*. Any picture is largely dominated by its bordering

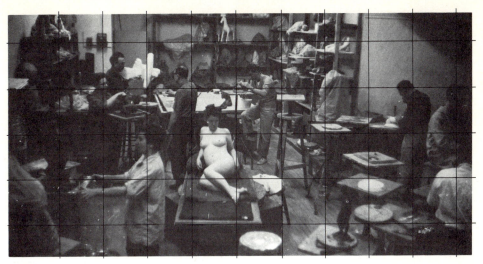

Figure 5-12 *(Gabriele Wunderlich)*

frame: that is its world. Whatever the center of interest, it exists only in relation to the placement of that frame.

EXERCISES

Using Figure 5-12, mark off *two* different rectangular picture frames. Do not begin until you are quite convinced that you have selected the best pictures possible.

DISCUSSION: When you have established your two pictures within the stated limits, compare them with those of your group. Discuss your reasons for choosing as you did. What might the purpose of each picture be? How would a given arrangement best satisfy that purpose?

WRITING: Translate each of your pictures into a sentence (word picture).

Picture 1: _____

_____

_____

Picture 2: _____

_____

_____

DISCUSSION: Read and compare the sentences within your group. Does each truly express the content and establish the boundaries of the picture it is supposed to reflect?

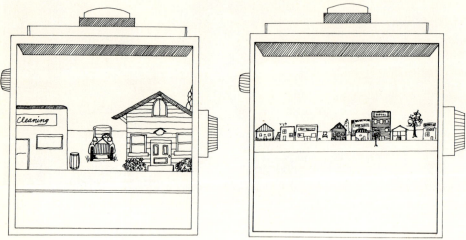

Figure 5-13   Figure 5-14

4.   *The relationship between things.* If one of your word pictures in the last exercise seemed to miss its mark, perhaps you neglected to distinguish between dominant and subordinate elements. As we have seen, a photographer achieves emphasis simply by moving his camera around. When we looked at our small-town street in search of a perfect composition, we came up with this tentative solution (Figure 5-13). And to establish an equivalent word picture we wrote the following:

Standing in the driveway of an old shingle-roofed house is a beautifully restored Model T Ford with a bright new canvas top.

Then, moving our camera much farther back, we decided on what is shown in Figure 5-14. And our word picture for this was:

Across a wide avenue, a row of variously shaped buildings rests beneath a vast expanse of sky.

In each sentence we managed to stress the same things as the corresponding picture. It was simple enough: We stated the important thing *last.* Technically labeled the *periodic sentence,* such a construction works on the principle that the final word gets the lion's share of attention. It is the climactic event.
     Another way of subordinating one detail to another (often as part of the climax-building order of a periodic sentence) is to present less important de-

tails in leaning sentences. For just as a leaning sentence has to lean on a whole sentence (to make a sentence plus), the idea it contains normally strikes us as weaker than the main idea that supports it.

I'll drive the station wagon,   if my father lets me.
    [SINGLE SENTENCE]   [LEANING SENTENCE]

She is a good conversationalist,   when she wants to be.
    [SINGLE SENTENCE]   [LEANING SENTENCE]

Jim is a wild man,   although he was raised in a pious family.
[SINGLE SENTENCE]   [LEANING SENTENCE]

Note that the leaning sentences seem a shade less significant than the parts that stand by themselves. However, if any doubt exists, complete and convincing emphasis can be achieved by placing the main idea (the single sentence) in the final (climactic) position, as follows:

If my father lets me, I'll drive the station wagon.

When she wants to be, she is a good conversationalist.

Although he was raised in a pious family, Jim is a wild man.

EXERCISES

1.   Rework each of the following idea clusters into a coherent sentence with clearly related parts and a strong climactic emphasis.

Example:
He passed Joe's Tacos.
It was lunchtime.
He stopped.
He was hungry.
He ate like a starving man.
He ordered five burritos.
Reworked·
He passed Joe's Tacos, and since it was lunchtime and he was hungry, he stopped and ordered five burritos and ate like a starving man.

a. The librarian smiled at her.
   She decided to ditch the lifeguard.
   She removed her makeup.
   She put on her glasses.

Rework: _____

_____

b. He hated history.
His eyelids drooped.
He read until dawn.

Rework: _____

_____

c. The surfer slipped off his board.
The big wave broke.
He pinwheeled into shore.

Rework: _____

_____

Figure 5-15 *(Gabriele Wunderlich)*

2.   Look at Figure 5-15. Describe this scene in one carefully constructed sentence.
Place most of the emphasis on its dominant elements.

Your sentence: _____

_____

_____

_____

DISCUSSION: Read all sentences in your group; compare their effectiveness.

5.   *The personal touch.* In the last analysis, most of our basic choices are a matter of "hunch" or "taste" or "instinct" or "temperament."

EXERCISES

Here are three completely different views (Figure 5-16 *a, b,* and *c*), all entitled "City Life." Which one strikes you as the most satisfactory expression of that subject, the most "right"?

DISCUSSION: Although this decision is a personal one, talk about it with the group.

a (Gabriele Wunderlich)

b (Harlan Hoffman)

c (Harlan Hoffman)

Figure 5-16. City life.

chapter 6

I AM A MOVIE CAMERA: THE PARAGRAPH

THE MOVIES

We stress the importance of writing good sentences because they are the bricks with which we build our written constructions. But one brick does not make a wall; likewise, few of our messages are as brief as this:

> As I look out my window I see an old clapboard hotel squeezed in between a brick grocery store with an iron roof and an ancient house with a screened porch; a farmer is passing—stepping around a tree growing out of the sidewalk.

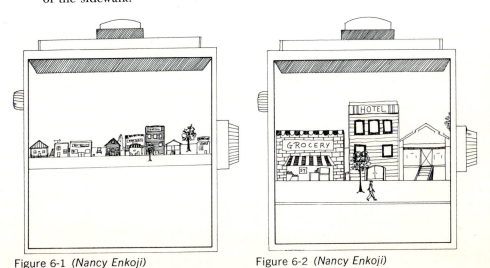

Figure 6-1 (*Nancy Enkoji*)   Figure 6-2 (*Nancy Enkoji*)

Figure 6-3

We compared that sentence to a snapshot, and we suggested that being limited to only one snapshot was, at best, uncomfortable. Most of us, like the writer in Chapter

5, would be tempted to expand the snapshot into a little movie. We would start with an overall view of the small-town street (Figure 6-1). Then we would show the most interesting section at closer range (Figure 6-2). Finally, we would present the best details in a series of close shots (Figure 6-3 *a* to *e*). Thus, instead of one snapshot, we might have five or more, all connected in such a way that they allow our viewer to look at the little street the way he would want to naturally—to grasp the whole idea first and then satisfy his curiosity about the parts. In other words, we would be connecting simple images into the kind of cumulative image that is characteristic of songs, poems, and scenes from plays.

"Connecting" is the key word here, for the mere placement of images one after another does not guarantee any kind of cumulative effect. One example of unconnected images may be found in many family albums. Usually the pictures are pasted in haphazardly—different faces in a variety of unexplained settings and in no perceivable order—so that while individual small images flicker in our memories, the effect of the whole collection is vague. Amateur moviemakers tend to achieve the same kind of vagueness. Though the individual scenes in a home movie may hold our interest, the scenes are usually fleeting in themselves and are rarely connected with the scenes that precede and follow them. Few amateurs bother to plan and edit their work to ensure that it gives its watchers a sense of flow or direction.

A good movie, like a good story, starts with a purpose and moves forward to make a point. And just as still pictures helped us to "see" sentences in the last chapter, movies, which are a continuous connecting up of still pictures, can give us insights into the nature of written composition as a whole—starting with paragraphs and moving into complete stories and articles.

Let us begin by comparing the "image units" of a film with those in a written composition.

THE FRAME

As Figure 6-4 shows, the smallest ingredient in a film is the individual *frame*. Just as individual words ("the", "off," "keep," "grass") usually escape our attention until they land in a sentence ("Keep off the grass"), the separate frames in a film exist only when they are perceived within a shot.

THE SHOT

The shot is to a film what the sentence is to a written composition: the most basic image unit. Technically, a shot is whatever a moviemaker gets on film between the time he presses the button and the time he releases it. For example, our snapshot (Figure 6-5) would be a movie shot if the cameraman had been able to pause and actually film the farmer as he moved (Figure 6-6).

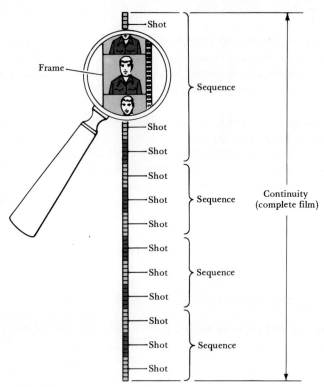

Frame = letter or word
Shot = sentence
Sequence = paragraph
Continuity = whole composition

Figure 6-4

Figure 6-5 *(Nancy Enkoji)*

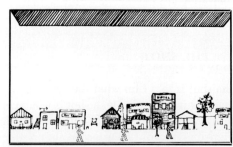

Figure 6-6 *(Nancy Enkoji)*

WORD PICTURE
As I look out my window I see an old clapboard hotel squeezed in between a brick grocery store with an iron roof and an ancient house with a
screened porch; a farmer is passing — stepping around a tree growing out
of the sidewalk.

In either case, the verbal equivalent of this visual experience is a *sentence*. Sometimes, of course, a movie shot may be long enough to do the work of more than one
sentence (Note that the word picture above is a long double sentence plus). In actual
practice, a shot may last anywhere from a second or less to thirty seconds or more.
An extremely brief shot may be the equivalent of the shortest sentence:

A car appeared.

A very expanded shot may contain several sentences:

He braked sharply at the curb, opened the car door, and got out slowly.
He started up the long flight of brick steps and paused twice as if to catch
his breath. When he reached the top, he happened to glance down just as
a man in overalls was climbing into his car.

However, the average film shot is between three seconds and ten seconds in
length, and it can normally be expressed in one sentence:

She paused to look into the fountain, and then she hurried on toward the
house.

EXERCISE
Look at Figures 6-7 and 6-8 as if each picture were a movie shot. Identify the main action
within the shot and then translate it into a sentence. Be sure to include enough descriptive detail. (Would it be best as a single sentence, a double sentence, a sentence plus,
or a double sentence plus? For a quick review of sentence types, turn back to page 94.)

_____

_____

_____

_____

_____

Figure 6-7 *(Harlan Hoffman)*

Figure 6-8

DISCUSSION: (1) Read your sentences aloud in your group. (2) As each sentence is read, try to see it as a moving image. Is it an effective image or could it be improved by the substitution of more accurate or more lively words? (3) Does the structure of the sentence fit the subject matter? (4) Does the descriptive detail (the extra comment) help or get in the way?

Movies *move,* and so does good writing. Most commonly within a single shot, this movement occurs within the boundaries of a "fixed frame," as if the camera is standing still and some action is moving in front of it (Figure 6-9).

The waiter slipped and pitched forward, and his tray full of lobster dinners sailed off his palm and crashed into the nearest occupied table.

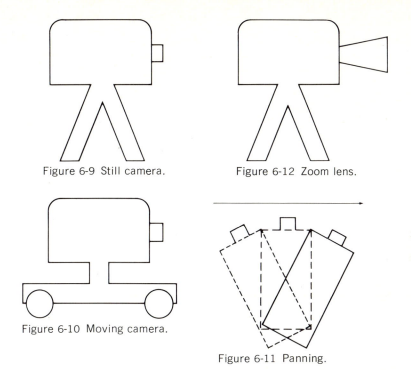

Figure 6-9 Still camera.   Figure 6-12 Zoom lens.

Figure 6-10 Moving camera.

Figure 6-11 Panning.

But often the primary movement is that of the camera itself moving along on a dolly. This is called a "tracking shot" (Figure 6-10).

> The merry-go-round was out of order, so he went back across the street; then, eyeing the new little excursion boat, he hurried down to the landing.

Sometimes the movement in a shot is mainly visual; the camera turns on its axis and sweeps from one point across to another. This is called "panning" (Figure 6-11).

> The love seat by the front door was tattered, but the sofa in the center of the room was impressive, and the leather club chair by the fireplace was magnificent.

Another kind of visual movement is the progressive magnification achieved by the zoom lens. This is called "zooming" (Figure 6-12).

> The girl who appeared in the doorway seemed tiny and unimportant until he noticed the costly elegance of her dress and then the quiet beauty of her features.

EXERCISE

Using Figure 6-13 as your resource, write four separate sentences about a restaurant. In each of your sentences, use one of the four techniques just discussed.

1. Camera in fixed position: _____

    _____

    _____

    _____

2. Camera moving on dolly (tracking): _____

    _____

    _____

3. Camera turning (panning): _____

    _____

    _____

Figure 6-13 *(Gabriele Wunderlich)*

_____

4.   Camera magnifying (zooming): _____

_____

_____

_____

DISCUSSION: (1) Read your sentences aloud to your group. (2) As each sentence is read, try to see it as if you were watching it on a movie screen. Is the technique used in each sentence the one most suitable to the subject matter? If not, why not?

THE SEQUENCE: MAKING CONNECTIONS

A *sequence* is any group of shots linked together in such a way that they make a single point or statement. A sequence is to a film what a paragraph is to a written composition or, sometimes, what a chapter is to a novel.

Before we proceed to the question of making a point, we must first consider the more basic problem of connecting the shots. This is a fascinating problem. Indeed, much of the art of movie making is no more than the art of juxtaposing shots, that is, getting them in the right sequence. To illustrate, look at Figure 6-14*a* and *b* as if it was two shots in immediate succession, *b* coming right after *a*. Study them for a moment; let them sink in. Note that the man *(b)* looks happy because the pretty girl *(a)* seems to be smiling at him. Then consider the arrangement shown in Figure 6-15*a* and *b*. Do you notice any difference in the man's expression? Perhaps a hint

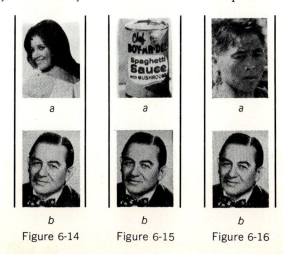

Figure 6-14   Figure 6-15   Figure 6-16

of hunger? And now, as he confronts a Vietnamese prisoner, his face seems to grow more somber (Figure 6-16*a* and *b*).

All this may help to explain why film actors sometimes have little to do but be *what* they are *where* they are and why the motion picture is often called a director's medium.

EXERCISES

1. Interpreting the three closely related pictures in Figures 6-17, 6-18, and 6-19 as movie shots, turn each into a sentence and connect it with the other two in the order that makes most sense to you.

    a. _____

    _____

    _____

    b. _____

    _____

    _____

    c. _____

    _____

    _____

DISCUSSION: Read your three connected sentences (shots) to your group. Notice how the placement of each sentence in relation to the others affects its meaning and emotional significance.

2. Write the following sentences into the slots below in any order:
    a. Just then he thought about his mother-in-law.
    b. The girl at the information desk was pretty.
    c. He went into the bar for a stiff drink.
    d. He clutched at his lucky rabbit's foot.
    e. The next day he was fired from his job.
    f. }
          } *Add two original sentences of your own.*
    g. }

Figure 6-17 *(Gabriele Wunderlich)*

Figure 6-18 *(Gabriele Wunderlich)*

Figure 6-19 *(Gabriele Wunderlich)*

_____

_____ It was half-past ten. _____

_____ He drove 80 miles per hour all the way to

the airport. _____

On the way his engine began to belch smoke. _____

_____.

He got to the airport an hour late. ___ _ _____

_____.

"You're acting like an idiot," his wife said. _____

_____.

DISCUSSION: (1) Read your completed sequence aloud to your group. (2) Consider the differences between sequences.

The specific way that one sentence is placed in relation to another has the same kind of effect as the placement of pictorial images. Each sentence, like each shot, seems contagious: it borrows something from the one that precedes it and sheds its influence on the one that follows.

THE SEQUENCE: MOVEMENT

In our discussion of the shot we stressed the importance of movement and the ways that it occurs: within the frame, by tracking, by panning, and by zooming. However, the movement that matters most is not that within a film's separate shots (its "sentences") but that within its whole sequences (its "paragraphs"). After all, a frozen still shot is often necessary if only to provide a moment of suspense before (and a contrast to) a shot full of lively movement. But an entire sequence *must* move. It must move us toward meaning—toward the sense of a completed image, and it must also move us into the next sequence, which builds upon that meaning. Thus, much of the problem of connecting is the problem of controlling the overall movement so that it succeeds in making a point.

EXERCISE

Below are eight totally unconnected sentences. Put any *six* of them into any sequence you choose.

Rules: You may not change the basic wording of these sentences, but you *may* add modifiers and connecting phrases. You may even add an extra sentence or two if you feel that this is absolutely essential to the development of your idea. *Write this on note-book paper.*

1. Cats like liver.
2. His mother wears tennis shoes.
3. Plastic cups should be kept dry.
4. The great enemy of clear language is insincerity.
5. Americans love "how-to" books.
6. If we don't all hang together, we will hang separately.
7. A real person is worth a million statues.
8. Red wine goes well with beef.

DISCUSSION: Read your sentence sequence aloud in your group. Take note of all the existing possibilities.

At the start of the last exercise you undoubtedly had to ponder those unconnected sentences for a while in search of some common denominator, some guiding idea among them that would marshal all the others into a meaningful order. (This is the kind of creative problem solving we discussed in Chapter 3.) And you probably began writing only after you found a way to make them all move along together in harmony.

Let's look at the way various shots can work together to give a film sequence this kind of harmonious movement.

First, consider these images:

1. A crying boy
2. A laughing man
3. An ugly shack
4. A full dinner plate
5. A shiny new car
6. A broken-down truck

Movement in Time

Some shots are linked together as a series of events happening in the course of time, like a story. If the above images were turned into shots (represented as sentences), they might be connected in this kind of *time* sequence:

Late in the evening a small boy comes out of an ugly old shack. Crying from hunger, he stands by his father's broken-down truck. Just then a shiny new car stops at the curb. The man inside is the boy's father. He takes the boy to a restaurant and sits there laughing as the boy plunges into a full dinner plate.

(*The point of this sequence:* The boy's evening started out badly but ended well.)

Movement in Space

Some shots are linked together so that the parts of a scene strike our attention one after another—as in a travelogue. Turned into shots, the images listed above might be connected in this kind of *space* arrangement:

> Parked outside an ugly shack are a shiny new car and a broken-down old truck. Through the open front door of the shack you can see a woman hunched over a full dinner plate on a TV tray. Next to her a man is laughing scornfully. Behind them, against a dirty white wall, a small boy is crying.

(*The point:* A glimpse of some poor people.)

Movement by Contrast

Some shots are linked up to show comparisons and contrasts. This can be done in two ways. First, the item-by-item contrast:

> Bill lives in an ugly shack. Jim lives in a mansion. Bill drives a broken-down truck. Jim has a shiny new car. Bill's son is always hungry. Jim's son can always expect a full dinner plate. Bill thinks a lot about suicide. Jim is usually laughing.

Second, the overall contrast:

> Bill lives in an ugly shack and drives a broken-down truck. His young son often goes hungry. Bill thinks a lot about suicide. But Jim occupies a mansion and drives a shiny new car, and his son can always count on a full dinner plate. Jim is usually laughing.

(*The point of each:* Rich people enjoy life, but poor people don't.)

Movement by Examples

Some shots are linked together solely to illustrate a general idea by furnishing a series of "for instances." Documentary films rely heavily on this method.

On Hill Street you will find small factories, model homes, and ugly old shacks all in a cluttered row. You can hear the laughter of busy workmen, the shouting of teen-age gangs, and the crying of hungry children. You may catch the aroma of catfish, then find this smell giving way to the scent of spicy refried beans, and then breathe in the hearty emanation of a dinner plate full of corned beef and cabbage. You will see shiny new cars and repairmen's vans and broken-down old trucks all parked together.

(*The point:* Hill Street is a neighborhood in transition.)

EXERCISE

Following the pattern above, write some brief sequences (in the form of connected sentences) based upon the following ideas and images:

1. A pretty girl
2. A bank
3. A police car
4. An old mortuary
5. A lame washerwoman
6. A horse
7. Death

Rules: You may add modifiers, connecting words, and even a few additional ideas, as we did. Try to use all the images stated above. And be sure to follow the method (the type of movement) prescribed for each sequence and to *state your point* at the end.

1. Movement in time (This is also called "narrative."):

Your sequence: _____

_____

_____

_____

_____

_____

Your Point: _____

2. Movement in space (This is also called "description."):

Your sequence: _____

_____

_____

_____

_____

_____

Your point: _____

3.   Movement by contrast (Show either an overall contrast or an item-by-item contrast.):

Your sequence: _____

_____

_____

_____

_____

Your point: _____

4.   Movement by examples:

Your sequence: _____

_____

_____

_____

_____

Your point: _____

DISCUSSION: (1) Read your sequences aloud in your group. (2) Does each one follow the prescribed pattern? If not, where does it deviate? (3) Does the stated point of each sequence seem to cover all the details *as they are presented?*

THE SEQUENCE: MAKING A POINT

In the last exercise you may have found that by concentrating on the type of movement each of your sequences was to follow, you were easily able to make a point that tied all your details together, or, conversely, you were able to pull your details together in such a way that you made a point. Most any time sequence (narrative) will add up to some kind of story that can be summarized in a brief topic sentence. And most space sequences (descriptions) deal with a place or person and can be tagged, "It was a filthy bedroom" or "He was a weird-looking character." Contrast sequences usually boil down to "This car is better than that car" or the like. And example sequences can hardly proceed until the thing being exemplified is so clear in our minds that it could readily be stated as a "point" or topic sentence.

However, while knowing what method to follow is half the battle, we usually do not begin with a method. Ordinarily we start with a notion of what we want to say and then proceed to find the best way to say it.

EXERCISE

Start with these two shots:

> It was a brick house in the suburbs.
> He drove a new car.

To these shots add five more of your own and develop all seven into a complete sequence (paragraph). Remember to connect them in the best possible order (time, space, contrast, or example) to make a clear and decisive point. State that point at the very end in the space allotted. (Try to imagine that each blank square contains a pictorial image, and explain it as a *shot* in your sentence on the adjoining line.)

SHOT SENTENCE

1. ☐ _____

   _____

   _____

2. ☐ _____

   _____

3. ☐ _____

4. ☐ _____

5. ☐ _____

6. ☐ _____

7. ☐ _____

Your point (topic sentence): _____

DISCUSSION: (1) Read your sequence aloud in your group. (2) In each sequence read, do all the shots hang together well? That is, do they seem to move along according to a discernible plan or pattern? (3) Does the stated point really cover all the details as they are presented? If not, what changes ought to be made? (Add more details? Change or delete some? Alter the topic sentence?) (4) Are the shots in this sequence varied enough to escape monotony? That is, are they all presented as if seen through a fixed frame, or do some reveal themselves inch by inch, as if the camera were tracking or panning or zooming?

In the last two exercises we stressed the *details* in the sequence and let the *point* (the topic sentence) more or less follow in their wake. However, most any screenwriter has his point clearly in mind before he seriously considers the details with which to build it. "Now this scene," he might say to himself, "will show how much trouble that dumb George has just getting to school in the morning." To illustrate this, he might work out the following sequence:

FILM SEQUENCE

Technical terms:

EXT = exterior (outside shot)

INT = interior (inside shot)

LONG SHOT: Camera takes in an entire house, group of people, etc.

MEDIUM SHOT: Camera catches one thing or person (sometimes two) with some detail but still stresses surroundings.

CLOSE SHOT: Camera shows a specific object (usually somebody's face) in intimate detail.

TOPIC IDEA: George has a lot of trouble getting to school.

SHOT 1.   EXT–LONG SHOT OF HOUSE FRONT–DAY

(George rushes out front door carrying books. He slips backward on the wet walkway, his head bouncing on the cement. His books fly off in all directions. After a moment he raises himself up onto his elbows.)

GEORGE

[MOANING AND SHAKING HIS HEAD]: What the hell!

SHOT 2.   EXT–LONG SHOT OF OPEN GARAGE

(George limps into garage where his old Studebaker is parked. He tosses his books into the back and then climbs into the front seat. After several attempts with the starter, the car's engine turns over and a great sooty cloud of exhaust belches out the pipe into camera.)

SOUND: Whir of starter, revved-up engine, clashing of gears.

(The garage door is propped up with a pole. The blast of the exhaust blows the pole away, and the garage door falls.)

SOUND: Crashing thud.

(The Studebaker backs out through the door, bursting it open like a drumhead.)

SOUND: Wood ripping and splintering.

(Without a second's pause, the car turns onto the avenue and speeds away.)

SHOT 3   INT—CAR—MEDIUM CLOSE SHOT—GEORGE

(George is gripping the steering wheel. The scenery flashing by indicates a high speed.)

GEORGE

[LOOKING AT HIS WATCH AND GRUMBLING]: Ten to nine.
Never make it!

SOUND: Car engine accelerating. Then a loud police siren.

GEORGE
[GASPING AND CLOSING HIS EYES WITH DESPAIR]: The fuzz!

SHOT 4.   EXT—LONG SHOT OF CAR AND MOTORCYCLE—POLICEMAN

(As the car slows to a stop, a policeman pulls up behind it and dismounts.)
SOUND: Loud motorcycle engine sputtering to silence.

POLICEMAN
[VIEWING THE CAR WITH DISTASTE AS HE WALKS SLOWLY TO THE DRIVER'S WINDOW
AND PEERS IN AT GEORGE]: What's the hurry, son? Say, aren't you the fellow I let
off with a warning last week?

SHOT 5. CLOSE SHOT—GEORGE

GEORGE

[HOPELESS, BUT WITH A SHEEPISH GRIN]: Gee, Mister Officer, I think you've got
me mixed up with some other guy.

FADE OUT

In an entertainment film like this one, there is normally no place for an explicit statement like "George has a lot of trouble getting to school." Here it is the writer's intention that we discover the point for ourselves by journeying through the details. But to make sure that our journey does end where he wishes it to— at our recognition of his topic idea—he must keep that idea firmly in mind every second of the way. Although he may have a hundred examples of George's ineptitude, in this sequence he must ruthlessly exclude any detail that does not clearly illustrate George's trouble in getting to school.

What is true in screenwriting is true in all effective writing: General ideas come first. For instance, a writer intent on showing the evils of smoking will start by jotting down such points as "Smoking is unhealthy," "It is expensive," and "It can be a social liability." Each of these topic sentences cries out for supporting details: the exact ways that smoking is harmful to health, the amount of money it actually costs, and the many ways that it can offend others. Of course, the writer who chooses this subject probably has bushels of facts at his fingertips, or he would never (unless he is a rash fool) plan such an article in the first place. But a writer who has *only* details and no topic ideas to contain them is bound to drift astray like a navigator without a compass.

What is true for the writer is also true for the reader. For him, details hang together better if he knows what they are supporting. (Notice that the sequence about George, although it lacks a "topic sentence," makes fairly clear in the first shot what is going to happen throughout; such "establishing shots" are common in films and do much of the work of a topic sentence in writing.) Since the reader is our prime concern as writers, it is a good idea to *begin* every paragraph with a topic sentence—even if it must later be removed or placed in some other position.

EXERCISES

1. Using the "George" sequence as your model, write an original film sequence. Remember to:
   a. Number each shot.
   b. Indicate interior (INT) or exterior (EXT).
   c. Indicate LONG SHOT, MEDIUM SHOT, or CLOSE SHOT.
   d. Indicate place of shot and characters involved.
   e. Indicate SOUND.
   f. Keep summaries of action separate from dialogue and accompanying stage directions.

   Write the sequence on notebook paper. *Begin with a topic sentence* and make sure that every supporting shot clearly illustrates your point.

   DISCUSSION: (1) Read all sequences aloud and try to imagine each as if it were on a movie screen. (2) Does each sequence clearly support its stated topic? (3) Is sufficient use made of SOUND and other descriptive detail? (4) Are CLOSE SHOTS used wherever appropriate? And MEDIUM and LONG SHOTS? (5) Do you like your sequence? Would it be effective if filmed? If not, how could it be improved?

2. Develop *one* of the following topic sentences into a paragraph by writing a supporting sentence on each of the allotted lines. Choose one:

   A car can be a giant headache.
   Dogs are often very useful pets.
   Falling in love is not all joys and blisses.

   Topic sentence: _____

   _____

   Details:

   a. _____

b. _____

_____

c. _____

_____

d. _____

e. _____

_____

DISCUSSION: Do all the details clearly support the topic sentence? Could any be changed or removed for greater effectiveness?

3.   The following paragraph lacks a topic sentence. Add one.

_____

_____

If the jacket fits perfectly, the pants will be too loose in the waist or hang too low in the crotch. If the pants fit well, the jacket will be too tight to button. And if you let the alterations man convince you that a few changes will be easy, be prepared to look like Frankenstein's monster, and plan on a two-week wait even though you need the suit next Friday night.

DISCUSSION: (1) Does each topic sentence clearly cover all the supporting details? Which ones are best? (2) How does this paragraph *move*—in time, in space, by constrast, or by examples?

4.   Write a brief paragraph starting with a topic sentence of your own.

Topic sentence: _____

_____

Details:
a. _____

_____

b. _____

_____

c. _____

_____

d. _____

_____

e. _____

_____

DISCUSSION: (1) Does each paragraph in your group meet all the stated requirements? Is the topic sentence both clear and adequate to cover all the details? Do all the details clearly support one idea, and is that the idea stated in the topic sentence? (2) How does each paragraph move?

THE SEQUENCE: LONG SHOT, MEDIUM SHOT, CLOSE SHOT

A few pages back we stated that general ideas come first and that masses of specific details are worth little without topic ideas to contain them.

The converse is just as true: General statements are scarcely worth considering unless they are backed up by specific details. If, in conversation with someone, you find yourself making some provocative statement like "The war in Vietnam was really caused by the Catholics," you must expect to be asked how and why. If you cannot come up with a few believable "for instances," you will be looked upon as rather foolish.

Actually, general ideas and specific details belong together. The movies furnish perhaps the best example of how this works. Typically a film will begin with a long shot to acquaint us with the locale of the action or the general mood of the story. Ordinarily such a shot makes a rather general statement. For example, look at Figure 6-20.

Although it is important for us to get our bearings, we are also naturally interested in knowing some details. Thus we want something like Figure 6-21. To satisfy our craving for detail, the moviemaker may now also give us something like Figure 6-22.

Probably the thing that will be most vividly remembered later is the close shot,

Figure 6-20 Long shot. *(Omikron)*

Figure 6-21 Detail. *(Omikron)*

Figure 6-22 Detail. *(Omikron)*

the specific detail. But without the general context provided in the long shot and the further interest aroused by the medium shot, that detail would not matter half so much. Have you ever seen a movie with nothing but close shots—all chins and noses and teeth? Some experimental filmmakers have tried it, and the result is always frustrating: we long to know the where and the why of these details that flicker by relentlessly. A film made up only of long shots is equally disturbing. Although we may enjoy watching a girl coming out of a distant cabin surrounded by large trees, it makes all the difference to us whether she is happy or sad, homely or pretty. In the final analysis, we need all these elements in constant interplay: general ideas (long shots), specific details (medium shots), and *very* specific details (close shots). Ever since D. W. Griffith, the pioneer film director, "invented" the close shot and established its rhythmic relationship with long and medium shots, we have come to expect this technique in every movie we see.

Good writers have always used it. In fact, Griffith got most of his filmmaking ideas out of the pages of Charles Dickens, one of whose novels he always carried to the studio. Every good writer is good mainly insofar as he knows what Dickens knew: (1) how to make general ideas persuasive by exemplifying them with plenty of vivid, interesting, and relevant details and (2) how to make details work together to deliver a message by harnessing them to some meaningful idea. Both things are essential.

The difference between movies and writing is even slimmer than we have suggested. Our main reason for using films as a guideline is to illustrate that writing improves substantially if it does what most films do naturally: They illustrate ideas with specifics. Since the film is a visual medium, it cannot help *showing* things. The most grievous error of the inexperienced writer is to show nothing but only to tell about something in the dullest, most general terms. For example:

> George had a lot of trouble getting to school. He had a rather nasty accident when he came out of the house. Afterward he had a great deal of trouble with his car. And once he got going, his driving left so much to be desired that the law got after him.

This paragraph is guaranteed to fade quickly from anybody's memory, mainly because it does not contain one really specific detail—not one of those telling, intimate frowns or shouts or sputters that always stick in the mind. Had the writer flexed his imagination and exercised his natural powers of observation, he might have caught our attention in the same way a film does. Indeed, he might have written a paragraph almost *exactly* like the movie sequence on page 125:

> My friend George had a lot of trouble getting to school today. Late, as usual, he came rushing out of the front door with an armload of books, and he slipped backward on the wet walkway, his head bouncing on the cement while his books flew off in all directions. It was several minutes before he managed to sit up and utter a few "What the hells!" Then he limped into the garage and climbed into his old Studebaker, tossing his

books into the back. It took several wheezing tries with the starter before George got the car's engine to turn over, and as he revved the motor it belched out a great sooty cloud of exhaust with such force that the pole supporting the garage door blew away, and the door dropped shut with a thud. Not noticing this, George ground the gears into reverse and backed straight out through the door, bursting it open like a drumhead. Without a second's pause, he turned onto the avenue and sped off as fast as he could. Minutes later he glanced at his watch. Ten to nine. "Never make it," he muttered. "Never make it!" He floored the accelerator and gripped the wheel. Suddenly the shriek of a police siren filled the air. "The fuzz," George gasped, closing his eyes in despair. As he pulled to a stop at the side of the road, he looked into the rearview mirror and saw the policeman wheeling up behind him and dismounting with his citation book. George caught the distaste in the policeman's eyes as he surveyed the shabby Studebaker before peering in. "What's the hurry, son?" was the man's opener, a brilliantly original line. "Say, aren't you the fellow I let off with a warning last week?" George felt himself turning pale, but he managed a stupid sheepish grin. "Gee, Mister Officer, I think you've got me mixed up with some other guy."

This is catchy writing, and the details are precisely what catch us. Hardly anything in the original script was changed or omitted, not even the sound effects. A few things were added—things that would have been visible to the camera and things that only writing can deal with explicitly, such as happenings within the mind. Most notably, the structure was identical.

> SHOT 1. EXT—LONG SHOT OF HOUSE FRONT—DAY
> SHOT 2. EXT—LONG SHOT OF OPEN GARAGE
> SHOT 3. INT—CAR—MEDIUM CLOSE SHOT—GEORGE
> SHOT 4. EXT—LONG SHOT OF CAR AND MOTORCYCLE—POLICEMAN
> SHOT 5. CLOSE SHOT—GEORGE

This same rhythmic interplay of the general and the specific—the long and the medium and the close—that would hold our interest on the screen is just as compelling on the printed page. And notice how specific a specific detail can be. To be told that someone is worried that he will be late is one thing, but to actually hear him saying, "Never make it. . . . Never make it!" is quite another. Now if that can be done in a movie, why not in writing?

EXERCISES

1. On a sheet of notebook paper, rewrite your original film sequence as a straight paragraph. Start with the same topic sentence and see how many of the same specific details (including sound effects, dialogue, etc.) you can retain. Also add any extra details that you think are necessary to complete the idea.

DISCUSSION: Read and evaluate the paragraphs within your group. Are there enough specific details in each one to sustain interest?

2. Write one very specific (CLOSE) statement on the line following each of the fairly general (MEDIUM) statements. For example:

    MEDIUM: Mary looked as if she wanted to kill Jim.

    CLOSE: She clenched her fists and got red in the face and said, "Phooey!"

    a. MEDIUM: Bill lost his money in the theater.

    CLOSE: _____

    _____

    b. MEDIUM: His car broke down on the freeway.

    CLOSE: _____

    _____

    c. MEDIUM: When he tried to kiss her good-night, she rudely rejected him.

    CLOSE: _____

    _____

    d. MEDIUM: After dessert, he knew he had eaten too much.

    CLOSE: _____

    _____

    e. MEDIUM: She did a bad job of carving the turkey.

    CLOSE: _____

    _____

DISCUSSION: (1) Read your sentences aloud in your group. (2) Is each CLOSE SHOT really a more specific extension of the MEDIUM SHOT, or does it stray off into a new idea? (3) Which of the details seems most effective? Most specific?

3. Complete the following paragraph by adding CLOSE SHOTS where indicated:

    LONG SHOT (general statement): As soon as the burglar jumped into his waiting car, the deputy started after him.

    MEDIUM: But at the first cross street the deputy had trouble with his car.

    CLOSE: _____

    _____

MEDIUM: As soon as he got moving again he was distracted by a radio call reporting further trouble in the district.

CLOSE: _____

_____

MEDIUM: The deputy put the call out of his mind, but at the next intersection he had to stop suddenly for a girl in the crosswalk, and she was even more distracting than the message had been.

CLOSE: _____

_____

MEDIUM: His heartbeat racing, he decided to let the burglar get away.
MEDIUM: He got out of his car and called to the girl.

CLOSE: _____

_____

DISCUSSION: Which of the paragraphs read in your group is the most enjoyable? Why?

NONFICTION: THE DOCUMENTARY FILM

Film is usually designated a "visual medium" and writing a "verbal medium." This implies that words function in some special, abstract way all their own. But as we have seen, words can also create pictures. Furthermore, it has been estimated that the greater portion of our sensory awareness is visual awareness. And so, if words are to touch us where we will feel them most strongly, they not only *can* make us see, they *must* make us see and also, whenever possible, make us hear and taste and smell and touch.

Thus far we have been stressing the story film, the kind that moves in time, to show how visual and other specific details may be used in writing. But not all films simply tell stories. The purpose of *documentary films* (travelogues, newsreels, and filmed articles) is usually to explain or analyze things—to develop ideas. Yet, being films, documentaries also make us see things. Often a topic sentence is stated by an off-screen narrator: "Our beautiful forests are being contaminated." This will be supported by a series of specific details: polluted streams, withered trees, despairing faces, and so on.

Obviously most nonfiction writing works in the same way—by supporting general ideas with examples. Yet the inexperienced or lazy writer, not finding himself faced with the necessity of carrying along a story, will often evade his responsibility to make things as clear as a film does. Typically he will write:

> Our beautiful forests are being contaminated. They are going to the dogs. They are being mistreated and dirtied up, and nobody seems to care what happens to them. They are "getting the business" because of human indifference and just plain neglect. It is a crying shame.

This paragraph is also a crying shame. It offers for our inspection no foul streams, no blighted trees, no dying animals. It only generalizes. It only repeats its topic idea four times until we are sick of it. We already read it once, we do not need to read it again and again. What we crave instead are clear "for instances." With a little thought, they are easy enough to supply, and they give an immense advantage to the writing.

EXERCISE

Select one of the following topic sentences and develop it with at least four specific examples. Make these examples as vivid as you can; make your reader hear and taste and smell and touch—and, above all, see. Be sure to support the underlined key word in each of your supporting details.

> Marriage has become extremely difficult.
> Life in our cities is increasingly uncomfortable.
> Tomorrow's transportation will be different.

Topic sentence: _____
Supporting details.

1. _____

   _____

2. _____

   _____

3. _____

   _____

4. _____

   _____

5. _____

_____

DISCUSSION: Which of the paragraphs in your group is best supported? Why?

Some documentary films go far beyond problems or conditions that can be simply illustrated with immediately relevant visual examples. Many films, often the "educational" kind, try to deal with abstract ideas. But again, being films, they also make us see things. For example, imagine a sequence beginning with this statement: "For all his goodness, man has always been enamored of war." To support this, a moviemaker might develop a systematic contrast by presenting a series of bright images of men doing noble things, each suddenly darkening and giving way to a picture from the annals of war's atrocities; he might show Socrates teaching the youth of Athens, the image then darkening (perhaps also splintering or crumbling) into a scene from the Peloponnesian War, or Einstein in his laboratory immediately followed by Hitler's panzers and death camps. Whenever a bit of imagination is drawn upon, even the most elusive of ideas can be clearly bodied forth.

Much writing, including the work of most philosophers, lies in this abstract realm. But no matter how obscure his subject, the skillful writer can usually make us *see* the meaning of his ideas just as a moviemaker can. Consider this paragraph by Erich Fromm.

Until now the One Man may have been a luxury, since the One World had not yet emerged. Now the One Man must emerge if the One World is to live. Historically speaking, this may be a step comparable with the great revolution which was constituted by the step from the worship of many gods to the One God—or the One No-God. This step was characterized by the idea that man must cease to serve idols, be they nature or the work of his own hands. Man has never yet achieved this aim. He changed the name of his idols and continued serving them. Yet he changed. He made some progress in understanding himself, and tremendous progress in understanding nature. He developed his reason and approached the frontiers of becoming fully human. Yet in this process he developed such destructive powers, that he may destroy civilization before the last step is taken toward constructing a new humanity.*

To back up his concept of the "One Man" emerging, Fromm gives us several fairly clear pictures: (1) man struggling to give up his many gods and turn to the One God; (2) man really only changing his gods' names; (3) man growing in his understanding

---

*Erich Fromm, *Beyond the Chains of Illusion,* Simon and Schuster, Inc. (Trident Press), New York, 1962. From pp. 186–187 of Pocket Books edition, 1962.

of himself; (4) man gaining mastery over nature; (5) man gaining in reason and moving toward the "fully human" frontier; and (6) man also building methods of destruction, perversely threatening to destroy the very civilization he has been making.

Although Fromm gives us no very specific details, in each example he allows us to picture "Man" (for which we naturally supply some simple human image) doing fairly understandable things. For "understanding nature" we are likely to envision someone working in a chemical laboratory, for "destructive powers" we are free to imagine a nuclear explosion, and so on. In addition, Fromm has strung these details together in a time sequence and has turned the passage into a kind of story. And telling a story is always the most interesting way to make any point.

EXERCISE

Select *one* of the following topic sentences and develop it with at least three good examples. Be as vivid and as interesting as you can be. Wherever possible, make your reader *see* things.

> Life is a tug-of-war between good and evil.
> Good and evil are only illusions.
> Love is man's only salvation.

Topic Sentence: _____
Supporting details:

1. _____

   _____

2. _____

   _____

3. _____

   _____

4. _____

   _____

DISCUSSION: Which of the paragraphs in your group is best supported? Why?

chapter 7

I AM A MOVIE CAMERA: THE CONTINUITY

THE THREE PARTS

The script for an entire movie is called the "continuity." That is a good word for any written composition—any *continuation* of one paragraph into another and another. But paragraphs do not just continue by themselves. Like the shots that go into a film sequence, they must be carefully *connected* to make a single point and to create a unified image.

In the last chapter we saw how this happens within the paragraph itself. A general idea or fact is stated as the topic sentence ("Young men are the best drivers"), and this is fleshed out with specific details ("Their reflexes are sharp," "They have good depth perception," etc.). The end result is that the topic idea *is* the paragraph— the final image we are meant to carry away. Yet it would not exist for us without the specifics that make it believable.

The whole continuity (whether film, story, article, or book) works in about the same way. A general idea is introduced and then fortified with enough specifics to enable it to drive its way across our attention threshold and into our memory as one solid, persuasive thing.

You are probably asking, "How can I possibly manage a dozen or more paragraphs without getting hopelessly entangled in all those specific details?" The answer: We never deal with all the details at once; we handle them only within their paragraphs, their topic containers, and we do this step by step, paragraph by paragraph. But before we even attempt this, we must take a backward step and decide on our overall meaning and organization.

Our first move in planning any continuity is to consider the number "three."

Hot—Warm—Cold   Rare—medium—well done

Life, liberty, and the pursuit of happiness . . .

Par 3   CODE THREE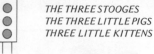
                                                 THE THREE STOOGES
                                                 THE THREE LITTLE PIGS
SEE NO EVIL   THREE LITTLE KITTENS
HEAR NO EVIL   Judicial—Executive—Legislative
SPEAK NO EVIL
                        The Three Musketeers
                        The Three Bears
The third degree!   HOLY TRINITY

                   The Triple Crown   the triple goddess

WW III   3–unit course   A THREE-YEAR HITCH

              PAST—PRESENT—FUTURE   3 PRIMARY COLORS

HUEY   ID
DEWEY   EGO   Breakfast   FOOD
LOOIE   Famous people die in threes SUPEREGO Lunch &   CLOTHING
                                                  Dinner   SHELTER
three feet in a yard
                                 3-flavored ice cream
small   MALE
MEDIUM   "COUNT THREE" FEMALE
LARGE   NEUTER
           24 hours a day   3-stage rocket   morning, noon, & night
           (8 X 3)
                                                 THREE ON A MATCH
Three break a tie vote . . . . Youth—Manhood—Age THREE IN A TUB

                                                 ALL MEN ARE MORTAL
First Name   Middle   Last   SOCRATES IS A MAN   A
                                                 SOCRATES IS MORTAL   B
        THREE-RING CIRCUS   Three bags of wool   C
father   Wine, woman, & song!
  mother   Three-speed shift
  child   THIRD REICH   "3 Big Hits!!"
                                                          BIRTH
       INDICATE YOUR FIRST, SECOND, & THIRD CHOICES   LIFE
ELEMENTARY   Three Ships of Columbus   BA   DEATH
JR. HIGH   MA
HIGH   3 polio shots   PhD   GAS, SOLID, LIQUID
               3 strikes 3-day measles
             3 tries   3 sets a match   THREE DIMENSIONS
FAITH, HOPE, & CHARITY
God, Honor, & Country   "The farmer had three daughters . . . . "
MENTAL, PHYSICAL, SPIRITUAL   3 wishes
Land, Sea, & Air   THREE SIMPLE STEPS
COFFEE, TEA OR MILK   NAME, RANK, SERIAL NUMBER   The earth is the third planet from the sun

        The life of Jesus: *Three* Wise Men followed the star . . . . Jesus was tempted
        three times . . . . He began teaching at thirty and taught for *three* years . . . .
        Peter denied him *three* times . . . . He fell down *three* times on the way to
        Golgotha . . . . *Three* nails were driven into him . . . . *Three* were crucified . . . .
        His crucifixion lasted *three* hours . . . . He died at *three* o'clock . . . . He was
        thirty–three years old at his death . . . . *Three* women watied at his tomb . . . .
                        He rose from the dead after *three* days.

THREE-TIME LOSER   *"The oldest fossil is three billion years old . . . . "*

  ACT ONE   BEGINNING   Exposition
                      ACT TWO   MIDDLE   Development
                      ACT THREE   END   Recapitulation

                        The third world

Figure 7-1

For of all the numbers, three is the one that sticks most steadfastly in the human mind. Indeed, its qualities seem almost magical at times. (Figure 7-1.)

The three-part item most pertinent to us here is *beginning—middle—end*. All the moving art forms seem inescapably bound up with this division into three phases.

In a stage play the phases are explicitly stated as the "three acts." The beginning, Act 1, gives us exposition; that is, it tells us who the characters are and acquaints us with their strengths and weaknesses, their needs and frustrations. By the time Act 1 is over we know the source of the conflict they are to engage in, which is the reason the playwright has brought them together in the first place. Act 2, the middle of the play, develops that conflict as far as it can possibly go. In the Greek tragedy *Oedipus Rex,* the hero struggles to find a man who murdered his own father and married his own mother. All along it is suggested that the culprit might be Oedipus himself, but he refuses to believe this. Yet in the end (technically, at the "climax") the facts are too persuasive, and he cries out, "I am that man!" Act 3, the end, resolves the conflict and "unties all the knots" (the French word used to say this is "dénouement"). Here Oedipus, having sworn to condemn the killer, condemns himself. Bluntly put, he gouges out his own eyes and goes into permanent exile.

In movies and television plays we are conditioned to beginning with a *teaser,* an attention-grabbing scene that comes even before the titles and credits. Sometimes the teaser is an entire first act, but more often it simply thrusts us into the main conflict of the story without delay and puts the detailed exposition off until later. Just as often the teaser is a provocative character sketch: it lets us know what kind of people to expect and sets the mood for comedy or tragedy or melodrama. Consider the opening scenes of the movies *Patton* and *The Graduate* and *Midnight Cowboy.* And what if our sequence about George were used as a teaser? By the end of it we would know enough to expect a slightly slapstick comedy about a perpetual loser, and we could make a good guess about the kind of conflict awaiting us. After the teaser, of course, most films and television plays stick closely to the three-act breakdown described in the last paragraph.

Novels and short stories generally follow the same dramatic pattern. Opening scenes and first chapters set the mood, establish the setting, and give us enough information about the characters to make us care what happens to them. What actually does happen is the "middle," and what this leads to is the "end."

Nor is music an exception. The traditional symphonic movement follows the sonata form, which is a division into (1) exposition, (2) development, and (3) recapitulation. Even the most lightweight popular songs tend to imitate this form.

Also consider the form of a typical business or technical report: (1) introduction, (2) discussion, (3) conclusions or (1) objectives, (2) data obtained, (3) recommendations or (1) statement of the problem, (2) experimental results, (3) summary and conclusion. The combinations of headings are endless, but the organization is almost always in three parts.

Literary essays and magazine articles are just as committed to this kind of structure. Consider these opening paragraphs from an article in *TV Guide:*

For Bob Cummings, the astrological portents were favorable, so he embarked on a project to buy property in Arkansas, where he will build a "small Disneyland" and shoot his new TV series.

For Sheila MacRae, the switch to TV from Broadway and night clubs came as a stunning surprise, but her astrologer knew it all the time. For comic Flip Wilson, the choice of a new personal manager was made by studying horoscopes of all the eligibles. For Barbara Eden, the I Dream of Jeannie genie, there was a chance meeting with actor Michael Ansara at the home of a Hollywood stargazer, who told them they were right for each other. Lo and behold, they were married.

The adventures of Bob, Sheila, Flip and Barbara reflect the growing influence of astrology on the television medium. Astrologer Katina Theodossiou, who uses computers from Time Pattern Research Institute to plot the movements of constellations, says 75 percent of the people now in TV are hipped on the stars. Some, of course, are having their horoscopes read only because it's fashionable—they like to jabber about their astrologers just as they once babbled about their psychiatrists. But fully one-third of TV's performing personalities, Miss Theodossiou tells you, are dead serious about this astrology. They will consult their favorite star-watcher before deciding when and where they will sign their contracts, what nights their shows should be aired, who their guests and co-workers should be, and what kind of shows they should do.

It's impossible to prove or disprove this estimate statistically, but New York's Joe Franklin, host of his own long-running, syndicated show, is convinced the figure is inflated. Franklin, who has done several shows on astrology, says many people in television consult astrologers because they find them stimulating—but don't really accept their advice. "I've found that they sometimes make decisions in accord with what the astrologers have told them, but they would have made these decisions anyway."*

Note the teaser beginning: we are plunged immediately into the world of Hollywood's astrology buffs. Only afterward does the author make a clear assertion about "the growing influence of astrology on the television medium." He completes this assertion at the end of the fourth paragraph with the quotation ending ". . . they would have made these decisions anyway." Thus, the article has begun. The purpose of this four-paragraph beginning is to state that although astrology has a hold on many people, its value is highly questionable. In the middle of this article (not reprinted here) the author develops his assertion by exploring many people's attitudes on astrology and by probing into its validity with increasing skepticism. The

* Martin Abramson, "Have You Consulted Your Friendly Astrologer Lately?" *TV Guide,* October 4, 1969. Reprinted with permission from *TV GUIDE* ® Magazine. Copyright © 1969 by Triangle Publications, Inc., Radnor, Pennsylvania.

end of the article (which we omit here) is a mild, whimsical, but still decisive put-down.

Thus the threes have it. To further stress our point, we ask you to imagine being offered only two choices, only two tries, only breakfast and lunch, only coffee and tea. And what about bowling with a two-holed ball or driving with a two-speed shift? Indeed, without that "third-and-final" option we always feel shortchanged, and never more so than when we are watching a movie or reading an article that does not give us a clear sense of beginning, middle, and end.

BUILDING A CONTINUITY: THE ABCs

To organize a continuity of your own, simply follow these ABC directions:

> A—Assert
> B—Build
> C—Conclude

We will consider each of these three steps in turn.

A—Assert

At the very beginning you must *assert* your main point and, by so doing, set the boundaries for your entire continuity. Thus, an assertion is to a longer composition what a topic sentence is to a paragraph. *Assert* means to state positively, affirm, or declare. In other words, if you mean to lure your reader into a journey of several pages or more, you must be willing to stick your neck out to get his attention.

For instance, imagine beginning an article with the question, "What about overweight people—won't they ever learn?" That one is sure to provoke a yawn, even from the fattest man on your block. But substitute something like "Overweight people are the victims of their early eating habits," and your reader is likely to respond, "All overweight people? What kind of eating habits? Why?" You will have whetted his curiosity and made him want to read on. Most real assertions, if they are clear and specific, have that kind of appeal. Of course, a reader's inclination to take up your challenge will depend considerably on his interest in your subject. but not entirely. Look at the following:

> Diaper rash can lead to serious mental disorders.

> The most important factor in a businessman's success is his wife's hair.

> Ex-jockeys make the most satisfactory husbands.

As far as we know, these statements are all untrue. Regardless of that, were you able to read any of them without a moment's pause or a twinge of curiosity?

By precept and example we have stated that an appealing assertion must be both *clear* and *specific.* Take this one: "American mores are indeterminately commingled with declining mythic prototype vectors." Here there seems to be an assertion, but what the devil is it all about? And now, consider the following:

> War is hell.
> Women are fickle.
> Americans are free.

These assertions seem clear enough, but none of them has the propulsion of a sip of warm milk. Frankly, they are all tiresome clichés. Here, a few specific details can make a world of difference.

> The experience of combat can sharpen the sense of life's meaning.

> A woman's inconsistency is often the product of a deep intelligence.

> For most Americans, real freedom is only a frustrating illusion.

Note that by adding interesting specifics, we have inadvertently changed the intent of our three original statements. But that is often the best way to deal with clichés—explode them. As someone once said, "When a thing is true so long that it becomes a truism, then it has probably turned false."

EXERCISES

1.   Read the following assertions.
       a. The depiction of military life in Hollywood movies is 90 percent hokum.
       b. In spite of the diet craze, men have always preferred women on the plump side.
       c. Modern mechanical conveniences create far more anxiety than comfort.
       d. Women's lib to the contrary, women have long enjoyed more real freedom than men.
       e. Television has had more impact on our attitudes and values than the discovery of atomic energy or the landings on the moon.

DISCUSSION: (1) Which of these assertions would you like to follow up by reading further? Why? (2) Apart from your preferences of subject matter, which of these seems *objectively* the best—the clearest and the most specific? Why? (3) Which is the weakest? Why?

2.   Consider these three clichés.
       a. The dog is man's best friend.
       b. Politics is a dirty business.
       c. Children should be seen and not heard.
       Think about it. Are the attributes of the canine species *that* impressive? Aren't most politicians more than just scheming opportunists? And what about children? Whether your inclination is to explode these clichés or to support and revitalize them, do so with enough specific details to transform them into clear and in-

teresting assertions. *Write your revised versions on the lines below:*

a. _____

b. _____

c. _____

DISCUSSION (1) Read your revised assertions aloud. (2) Take each transformed cliché in turn. Which of those in your group comes through as the catchiest? Consider why.

3.   Look at Figures 7-2, 7-3, 7-4, and 7-5. Giving free rein to your creative imagination, connect these four pictures into a brief first act or teaser which will lay the

Figure 7-2

Figure 7-3 *(Gabriele Wunderlich)*   Figure 7-4   Figure 7-5 *(Gabriele Wunderlich)*

groundwork for an extended conflict; that is, develop the *beginning* situation of a film or play. You may link these pictures up in any order that suits you. (For a brief review of this picture-connecting process, turn back to Chapter 3, pages 68–69). *Explain your first act or teaser with as much detail as you think necessary. Do this in the space below.*

_____

_____

_____

_____

_____

_____

DISCUSSION   (1) Read your summaries aloud. (2) Which one intrigues you most? That is, which beginning situation most stimulates you to ask, "What happened then?" (3) Which one strikes you as the most imaginative and makes the cleverest use of all the existing possibilities? (4) Informally discuss the ways in which these opening scenes might be built upon in later scenes.

B—Build

Only after you have formulated your assertion can you *build* your continuity. You do this by adding specific "for instances" in almost the same way that you develop a topic sentence into a paragraph. Let us illustrate this by starting with an already familiar assertion:

Tomorrow's transportation will be different.

As we confront this statement our first question must be, Is it broad enough to carry the burden of *many* supporting details? To test it, we must consider all the possible subitems that add up to our main subject, transportation. First, we think of automobiles, then railroads, airplanes, and ships. What about separating cargo vehicles from passenger carriers?

Thus, a moment's reflection has persuaded us that we have enough ideas for several paragraphs, hence enough material to begin building. Our next step is to lay this material out in the form of a *rough outline.* To do this, we simply list our subitems and jot down any features that illustrate the key idea in our assertion—in this case, "differences."

TOMORROW'S TRANSPORTATION WILL BE DIFFERENT:

SUBITEM		DIFFERENT IN WHAT WAY?
1.	Cars	*Smaller — clean engines —*
2.	Trains	*Used by all — fast — monorail*
3.	Airplanes	*Will move in any direction*
4.	Ships	*Large but fast — hydrofoils*

Now, to see just how far we have come, let us turn a few of our rough jottings into statements. In our first category alone (cars) we have already isolated the following possibilities:

1. Because of the heavily crowded roads, cars will be smaller and capable of being connected with one another into "instant buses" for long commuting.

2. Cars will be powered by nonpolluting engines—steam, turbine, Wankel, electric, etc.

3. Cars will have truly effective safety devices as well as centrally controlled speed monitors.

4. Since most commuting will be done in improved public vehicles, private cars will normally be rented or leased for the occasion, not owned.

Thus our few hasty notes on cars have spawned at least four interesting topic ideas (none of which is likely to please today's young car buff). But before proceeding to trains, we are well advised to pause at this point and reconsider our original assertion.

Remember, a good assertion is as specific as it can be. And in view of the things we have said about cars, is "Tomorrow's transportation will be different" really the best we can do? Actually each of our four statements refers to some increase in *efficiency*. Smaller cars will be simpler to handle, will take up less space, and will be easy to link up in commuter convoys. New engines will keep the air clean. Safety engineering will eliminate accidents. Renting and leasing will match need with cost. Thus we are talking about mechanical efficiency, social efficiency, and financial efficiency. And if our thoughts on trains and planes and ships prove roughly consistent with these ideas, we may well find that our assertion has become "Tomorrow's transportation will be vastly more efficient."

What about that vague word "tomorrow"? Are we talking about a hundred years from now? Most likely not. At the outside, judging from our guesses about cars, thirty or forty years seems a more plausible projection. Why not settle upon that much-discussed year 2001 and be done with it? Thus, our tentatively final assertion might read:

Transportation will be totally efficient by 2001.

Now we are ready to go back to our rough outline to see how many more good statements emerge and to test the capacity of our new (and catchier) assertion to contain all of them. Let us assume that we have done this and that all but a couple of our statements clearly illustrate transportation efficiency by 2001. If this occurs, we have no choice but to ruthlessly eliminate the two misfits.

Now that our materials are all laid out and waiting, we are almost ready to build in earnest. But first let us examine our early blueprint one more time. Is our original sequence of events really the best one? Should we start with cars and move to trains, then to airplanes, and finally to ships? This is an important matter. As we pointed out in Chapter 6, each sequence in a continuity has one main purpose: to move its audience forward to the next sequence. Many instructors of writing state that the best arrangement is always one that moves progressively *from less important to more important points,* an arrangement ever dangling a new excitement in front of the reader's nose. We think this is a sound rule, but it cries out for a little further explanation. How are trains more important than cars or ships than airplanes? Obviously the scale of importance, the basis of comparison, is something that the writer must provide as he connects the various parts of his continuity and in the way that he connects them. So this review of our first outline must be primarily an inquiry into these connections.

Connections are called "transitions." Between sentences, transitions are made with such expressions as "and," "however," "furthermore," "on the other hand," "for example," and so on. But transitions between longer units—paragraphs or related groups of them—usually require more explicit detail. For convenience, we shall treat them as separate smaller paragraphs, like slabs of mortar between the bricks of the construction. To illustrate, let us consider our article on transportation as it now stands:

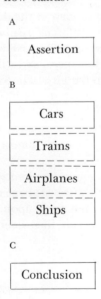

A

| Assertion |

B

| Cars |
| Trains |
| Airplanes |
| Ships |

C

| Conclusion |

Clearly, our first major transition will have to fall between our main assertion and our first (and least-important) subsection, cars. Assuming that we have already begun by planning an introductory paragraph that forcefully advances that assertion, how do we make this first shift? Here is one suggestion:

A

> (Introductory paragraph which states our assertion)

TRANSITION

> Most of us think first of the private automobile. And all the talk about crowded highways, air pollution, and safety hazards points to needed changes. In fact, present safety features and smog devices as well as the continuing trend to smaller vehicles already give us a preview of the car of 2001.

B

> (First supporting paragraph: cars)
> That car will be small, all right. Early projections suggest that it will be about half the size of the present Volkswagen. It will weigh. . . .

Thus we have smoothly bridged the gap between a general thing (transportation) and a specific one (cars) and moved from A to B. Of course our transition paragraph is rather sketchy as it now stands, but the important thing is to *set down the main idea,* and that we have done. Later, when we get around to revising our entire article, we will probably want to expand and embellish this paragraph into something like the following:

> For most of us the first form of transportation that comes to mind is the private automobile. The ever more gruesome accident figures together with the dire warnings of the ecologically minded leave little room for doubt that this, our most beloved conveyance, is going to get the lion's share of modification from now on. Some say that the automobile must change or die. But in a sense it is already dying, that two-ton, smog-spewing, chrome-festooned monster we have so long regarded as a necessity. Almost daily we read of some exotic new engine or fuel, or some clever device for cushioning our bodies in a crash (while denying us freedom of movement the rest of the time), or some bizarre new vehicle from Japan or Germany—invariably smaller than we would like. These and other intriguing novelties may all be regarded as scattered forecasts of the kind of car that will emerge by 2001.

And now let us supply our next main transition, from cars to trains. Here is another rough example:

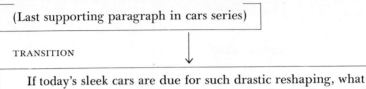

(Last supporting paragraph in cars series)

TRANSITION

If today's sleek cars are due for such drastic reshaping, what about our musty old trains? But look again: In the dreams of transportation engineers, the "railroad" is as far from those familiar boxy relics of the nineteenth century as a computer is from an abacus.

(First supporting paragraph: trains)
Indeed, high-speed, ultralightweight, monorail express trains will be the main arteries of our social and commercial existence. . . .

Again we have fused our transition directly into our first supporting idea, this time the future prevalence of trains. And note that we have managed to move from a "less" to a "more."

To achieve the same thing with airplanes, we might proceed as follows:

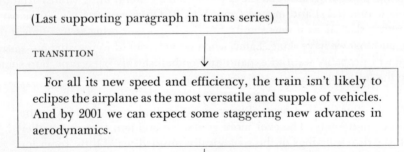

(Last supporting paragraph in trains series)

TRANSITION

For all its new speed and efficiency, the train isn't likely to eclipse the airplane as the most versatile and supple of vehicles. And by 2001 we can expect some staggering new advances in aerodynamics.

(First supporting paragraph: airplanes)
Imagine a plane that can move in any direction from 0 miles per hour to supersonic speeds. . . .

And again we have shifted from a "less" to a "more." Now let us try it with ships:

(Last supporting paragraph in airplanes series)

TRANSITION

But however dazzling the advances in efficiency predicted for cars and trains and airplanes, later ages will probably remember 2001 as the year that launched the century of the ship. This may sound paradoxical, as waterborne vessels are among the most ancient of devices. Yet today we are witnessing a breakthrough in ocean travel that makes the invention of the steam engine seem trivial by comparison.

(First supporting paragraph: ships)
The key word is speed, the kind of speed a hydrofoil can provide. Envision an entire warehouse of merchandise or the populace of a typical Midwestern town moving across the Atlantic Ocean in about a day. . . .

And so our progressive movement from least to most important has been completed. Only our concluding paragraph remains to be written. But saving that for later consideration, let us quickly review the entire process so far.

A

Introductory paragraph
(presents assertion)

B

First transition paragraph

Cars (first paragraph)
Cars (second paragraph)
Cars (third paragraph)

Second transition paragraph

Trains (first paragraph)
Trains (second paragraph)
Trains (third paragraph)

Third transition paragraph

| Airplanes (first paragraph) |
| Airplanes (second paragraph) |

| Fourth transition paragraph |

| Ships (first paragraph) |
| Ships (second paragraph) |

C

| Concluding paragraph |

We should now be asking ourselves, "Does this forward movement really *work?* Is it convincing? Does it bear out our assertion?" If it does not, we may have to reconsider both our assertion and our transitions or even change the basic order of our four subsections and then devise new transitions to accommodate them. But if we accept our scheme as presently outlined, then we are ready to forge ahead.

Our actual building is simply a matter of getting the article written. Again we are back to that first paragraph which will introduce our main idea. Most of our work here is over, as we are already sure of the assertion which is to be the heart of that paragraph. The problem is how to present it. Once more, we must make it a kind of teaser. We must entice our reader into joining us. We must even mystify him a bit and steadfastly resist the temptation to give away our specific details too soon (our transitions and subsections, as we have plotted them out, will do this later for maximum effect).

One way to grab our reader is to approach our assertion backward. Instead of mentioning the future outright, we can start by talking about the past.

"Travel" is a romantic word. It calls up vistas of moonlit ocean crossings and evokes the stirring clickety-clack of the railroad with its sumptuous meals served on white linen while scenic panoramas sweep by a window away. And those of us who veer off the freeway sometimes get a taste of highway travel the way it used to be: the rambling odyssey through unknown towns, the lure of little side roads, and the unscheduled lunch stops at quaint cafés. Yet these mellow images also suggest slowness and inefficiency, and there's the rub. For the spirit of the time demands that everything be efficient, and that spirit resides in most of us. Is any scenic view worth more than the assurance that we will travel safely and cheaply and arrive in time to keep our appointment in an uncontaminated environment? Whatever our answer, most existing methods of travel are rapidly being modified to meet just such standards. And however chilling some of the implications, experts predict that 2001 will mark the beginning of total efficiency in transportation.

The virtue of this stress on the past is that it puts the present or (in this case) the future in sharp relief. And almost any subject seems more interesting when compared with something else than when it is viewed in isolation.

Another intriguing way to begin an article is to tell a story. In the present instance, an account of somebody's experience on a monorail train or a hydrofoil boat could be most effective in introducing the subject and in setting the desired tone. A description could be just as appropriate—perhaps a mood-setting glimpse of the interior of a sleek new 747 jet and the faces of its strapped-in passengers. Sometimes a provocative quotation from someone is the ideal teaser. Actually, the possibilities are unlimited.

But whatever method we adopt, we must be sure that our already-calculated assertion comes at the end of the introduction. A good teaser creates suspense; it prompts the reader to wonder, "What is he getting at?" We must not tip our hand until the last possible moment.

And now, having completed our main introduction and our first transition, we are ready to develop our first supporting idea into a full-fleshed paragraph. In fact, we are ready to develop the entire article. As we do this we will bear in mind that each paragraph—each sequence in any continuity—must move the reader along to the next. If we let any one paragraph drift away from its purpose, lose *unity,* fail to present enough *detail* to validate the main point, or neglect to establish a *coherent* line of movement, then we are in danger of losing our reader for good.

Again, as we stated in Chapter 6, the four main types of paragraph or film-sequence movement are:

1.   Movement in *time* (the narrative—telling a *story*)
2.   Movement in *space* (*description*—sight, sound, smell, touch, and feel)
3.   Movement by *contrast* (the overall contrast or the item-by-item contrast)
4.   Movement by *examples* (the series of "for instances")

Additional and related types of paragraph movement include:

5.   Movement by *analysis* (breaking something up into its parts, as in an outline).
     This is a form of movement by example. It is also akin to description, but instead of moving the reader through physical space it moves him through a kind of mental space. Here is a brief example:

     There are three basic kinds of matches. In the first group are paper book matches, designed by advertisers for smokers. In the second group are wooden utility matches, a must for campers and pyromaniacs. In the final category we may lump together all those fancy imported "gift" matches—some tiny, some a foot long, and some brightly colored—which seem to have but one purpose: to sit on display.

6.   Movement by *process analysis.* This is like a narrative because it is an analysis (and enumeration) of events in a time sequence. It is the principal method of cookbooks and do-it-yourself manuals. For example:

You can make a wine cooler by following these four simple steps: First, fill an eight-ounce glass half full of Seven-up. Second, fill the rest of the glass with pink chablis wine. Third, add ice. Fourth, stir it briskly for five seconds. Now drink up!

Normally, one kind of technique or movement will be implicit in the topic idea awaiting development.

TOPIC SENTENCE	MOST OBVIOUS METHOD
Riding the bus can be a nasty experience.	Narrative
Pulik are friendlier than spaniels.	Contrast
The car of 2001 will be very tiny.	Description
This pill cures colds five ways.	Process analysis

(For a more detailed investigation of paragraph techniques, turn to Chapter 10. Also review our basic concept of the paragraph as film sequence in Chapter 6.)

C—Conclude

To conclude is to round things off, to bring a sense of completion. Remember, a play ends with a resolution (a dénouement or "untying of knots"), a symphonic movement with a recapitulation (a swingback full circle to the original theme), and a technical report with a summary or set of recommendations.

The concluding paragraph of the article on transportation (or any article) ought to do all these things. It may be regarded as a kind of final transition that swings back to the original assertion and beyond. It must tell the reader, "I promised I would say these things, and see, I have said them!" But just as important, it should present some parting generalization, some all-too-human assessment of further implications. The reader will welcome a touch of editorializing after pages and pages of neutral facts.

There are as many ways to conclude as to begin, but here is a possibility.

> (Last supporting paragraph in ships series)

CONCLUSION

> Will wonders never cease? Probably not. We could go on about space-age elevators, moving sidewalks, and the rebirth of the dirigible. We could speculate on still-undreamed-of scientific breakthroughs and touch on spooky things like the electronic "translation" of human beings into receptacles half-way around the world. But we trust we have drawn a fairly credible outline of that world awaiting us around the next

corner. Of course, one big question remains: Do we really want that world? Efficiency means capacity to produce results, and it can be argued that constant movement from one place to another is less productive for human beings than simply being in one place. Most of us function best when we feel "at home" somewhere at least long enough to look around at the sights, take a little stroll, and enjoy a meal and some good conversation. In any case, we owe it to ourselves to ask whether or not somebody else's Tomorrowland is the land of *our* heart's desire. If we don't ask, who will?

Although the article now seems complete, a final problem remains: its *style.*

This is the time to read the whole thing through to make sure that no rough spots remain, like heaps of rubble, to clog the flow of the argument. Are all the words the right ones? Are the sentences clear, smooth, and sufficiently varied to avoid monotony? Does each paragraph create a solid, persuasive image that builds upon the last one and propels the reader into the next? Most important, do all details add up to a single *total image* that gives us that sense of *oneness* we get from a well-made picture? To ensure oneness, we must rewrite painstakingly. And considering that our really hard work is already behind us, rewriting can be a most rewarding task. Just as a lovely dress and hairdo can turn a plain girl into a beauty, a careful revision can make the difference between mediocrity and excellence.

A COMPREHENSIVE EXERCISE

Taking one step at a time, write an entire article.

1. Select *one* of the following assertions:

    Our <u>cities</u> are being | destroyed |

    <u>Television shows</u> are | intellectually damaging |

    The <u>tax laws</u> are | unjust |

    <u>Clothing</u> is a | key to personality |

    Most of our <u>problems</u> could be solved | by love |

    Or complete your own assertion by filling in the blanks.

    _____ is the most | rewarding | of all hobbies.

A _____ is the most [entertaining] pet.

A _____ makes the most [satisfactory] girl friend/boyfriend (choose one).

_____ is the most [difficult] occupation.

Write the assertion you have selected in the line below.

_____

2. Using the lined form below, divide your subject into four subsections. (In each of the above assertions, your subject has been underlined.)

SUBSECTIONS   IN WHAT WAY? (KEY IDEA)

a. _____   _____

b. _____   _____

c. _____   _____

d. _____   _____

3. Now, using the same lined form, apply the key idea of your assertion ([boxed]) to each of your subsections by jotting down features that illustrate this key idea. (Destroyed in what way? Rewarding in what way?) For an example of this process turn back to page 147.

4. Turn your rough jottings into complete statements.

Subsection a (Identify it.): _____

Supporting statements (See page 147 for examples.):

_____

_____

_____

_____

Subsection b (Identify it.): _____

Supporting statements: _____

_____

_____

_____

_____

_____

Subsection *c* (Identify it.): _____

Supporting statements: _____

_____

_____

_____

_____

Subsection *d* (Identify it.): _____

Supporting statements: _____

_____

_____

_____

_____

5. Consider whether your statements clearly support your original key idea or whether they suggest that it ought to be modified and made more specific. In other words, could you further narrow your assertion as we narrowed ours by changing "different" to "efficient" and "tomorrow" to "2001"? If so, rewrite it here.

_____

_____

Check to see that all your supporting statements clearly back up your revised and narrowed assertion. If one or two do not, *eliminate them.*

6. By now you should have an assertion, about four subsections to illustrate it, and a series of statements showing how your key idea applies to each subsection. But are you sure that your subsections are in the proper sequence? That is, do they move from least to most important? If not, change their order. Then test this new arrangement by providing transition paragraphs.

   Do your transitions clearly establish a progression from least to most important? If they do not, rework them. If they do, you are ready to begin writing.

Assertion

(Now plot out the main idea of this transition.)

↓

Transition 1: _____
_____
_____
_____
_____

↓

Subsection *a*

↓

Transition 2: _____
_____
_____
_____
_____

↓

Subsection *b*

Transition 3: _____

_____

_____

_____

_____

↓

Subsection *c*

↓

Transition 4: _____

_____

_____

_____

_____

↓

Subsection *d*

7. *Homework assignment:* Using notebook paper, begin by writing a complete introductory paragraph. Some of the possibilities, as discussed on pages 152–153, are past versus present, narrative, description, and quotations. Be sure to save your explicit assertion — the actual statement of it — for the very end of the paragraph. Keep your reader wondering, "What is he getting at?"

8. Turn your rough first transition into a well-written paragraph. (See page 149 for one example, followed by a more polished version of the same paragraph.) Take care to provide a smooth interface between your introduction and the topic sentence of your first subsection.

9. Develop the topic sentence of each subsection into an effective paragraph. (Should it be predominantly narrative, description, comparison, example, analysis, or process analysis? See pages 153–154.) Check for unity, adequacy of detail, and a coherent line of movement.

10. As you move along, keep working on your transition paragraphs. Smoothly bridge each gap and reinforce the progression from least to most important.

11.   Now write an effective conclusion. (See pages 154–155 for ideas and an example.)

12.   Finally, reread everything you have written, and start revising. When you have finished, *revise again.* Make it brilliant.

DISCUSSION: (1) When you have completed your article, read it aloud in your group. (2) After each article is read, consider its overall effect. Does it convey a clear sense of beginning, middle, and end (the ABCs)? Does it have *unity?* If it seems to lack unity, go back to its basic assertion to see if it is specific enough to be *about one thing* yet broad enough to be dividable into clearly illustrative subsections. (Remember, without the anchoring security of such an assertion, a writer will almost surely find himself drifting.) If the assertion seems good, do the subsections clearly point back to its key idea, or has the author failed to eliminate some irrelevant points? (3) Is the article's *total image* forceful and persuasive? In other words, does each supporting paragraph have enough good *detail* to create a solid subimage that builds upon those preceding it and leads naturally into those following it? Do all the images add up to one thing? (4) It it continuously interesting? Do all the *transitions* help to sustain a clear progression from least to most important? (5) What about *style?* Is the actual language of the article an asset or a liability? Why? (6) Is the article really pleasurable? Sometimes a writer seems to do all the right things, and he is still as dull as dishwater. If this happens in your group, review the rules of this assignment and then go back over the article in question and try to pinpoint any problems. What changes might be made? Also, try to find the reasons for obvious successes.

BACK TO THE MOVIES

If, during the last exercise, you occasionally drifted into the swamp of wordy vagueness by using lazy generalities instead of clear images, you are ready to go back to the movies. Again, the incorrigible way films have of explaining everything with pictures can be profitably applied to most any form of writing.

The reverse is equally true: the rules we have recommended for writing an article generally hold up for movies. With certain obvious modifications, our diagram of an article (pages 151–152) could be safely followed in the preparation of almost any documentary film. For example:

A (ASSERT)

Introduction: a brief sequence to tease or set a mood or make a clear visual statement. The main assertion, spoken by a NARRATOR, is overlaid upon these pictures. It should be brief, and at the end of the sequence.

↓

B (BUILD)

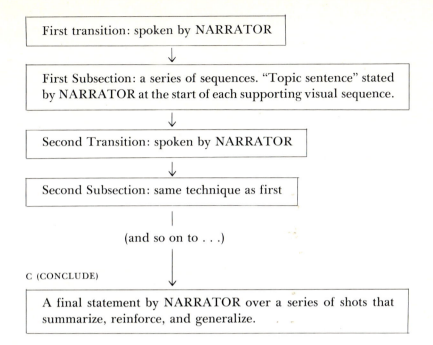

First transition: spoken by NARRATOR

↓

First Subsection: a series of sequences. "Topic sentence" stated by NARRATOR at the start of each supporting visual sequence.

↓

Second Transition: spoken by NARRATOR

↓

Second Subsection: same technique as first

|

(and so on to . . .)

C (CONCLUDE)

↓

A final statement by NARRATOR over a series of shots that summarize, reinforce, and generalize.

EXERCISE A

Just for fun (we trust), sketch out a short documentary film by combining the still pictures in group A. Each picture is to represent a *shot* and each connected group of pictures a *sequence*.

1. Examine all the pictures in group A (Figure 7-6, pages 165 and 167) for thematic possibilities. How can they be related to one another? What do they seem to be saying to you?

2. Cut out all the pictures with scissors (if no scissors are available, tear them out carefully) and begin moving them around on the worksheet (pages 161–176). Make this a creative exploration: do not jump at the first and most obvious sequence structure that comes to mind (it is usually the cliché), but grope for the one that will best express your individual ideas and feelings.
    [Alternative Approach *(If preferred, this approach should be adopted by the entire class.):* Instead of separating the pictures, simply write the number of each one selected into the square on the worksheet where you want to place it. The advantage of this method is that it will enable you to read your completed continuity to a large number of people at one time simply by stating a number and giving your audience a moment to locate the picture to which it corresponds. The disadvantage of this method is that it deprives you of the creative pleasure of physically juggling the pictures.]

3. This is an all-at-once operation. While you are deciding on a way to combine these pictures, you must also be thinking out a governing assertion, a few main transitions, and a series of topic statements all to be written into the boxes assigned on the worksheet. As soon as possible, jot down your main ideas on notebook paper to see how they work together. Do not paste in any pictures until you are quite sure.

4. Ready? Now turn to the instructions on the worksheet.

WORKSHEET
FOR GROUP A

INSTRUCTIONS: We have provided more blank picture squares than you will need, so *be selective.* Your subselections should vary in length; some may use all three of the possible sequences allotted, others only one or two. Some of your sequences will require more shots than others. And just as one movie shot can take more time than another, you may interpret some of these pictures as brief shots, others as very extended.

Be sure that each of your written inserts has enough clarity and detail to explain and "cover" the picture shots and sequences adjoining it.

Now begin pasting in your pictures and writing in your narrator's explanations.

A │ Introductory sequence:

NARRATOR (main assertion): _____

_____

_____

_____

_____

_____

Transition into first subsection — NARRATOR: _____

_____

_____

_____

_____

_____

(First subsection)

B   Sequence 1:

NARRATOR (topic statement and commentary): _____

_____

_____

_____

_____

_____

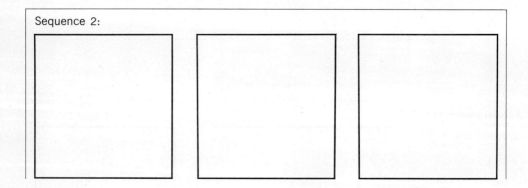

Sequence 2:

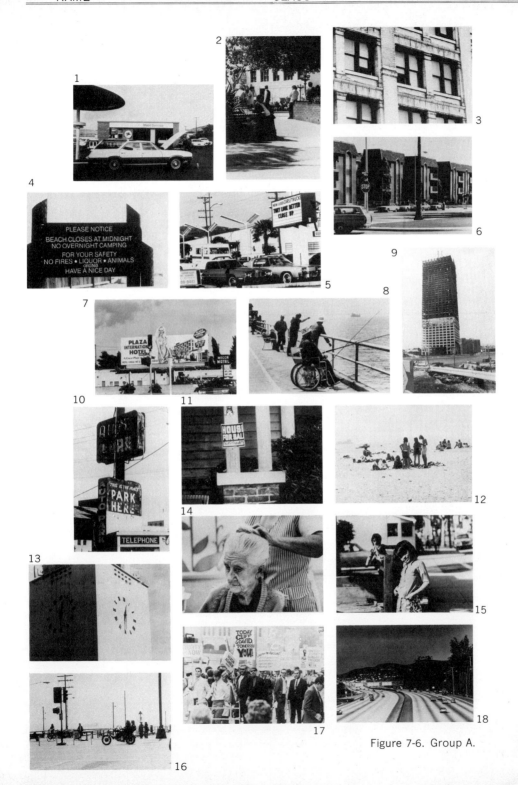

Figure 7-6. Group A.

Figure 7-6. *Continued.*

NARRATOR: _____

_____

_____

_____

_____

_____

Sequence 3:

NARRATOR: _____

_____

_____

_____

_____

_____

↓

Transition into second subsection — NARRATOR: _____

_____

_____

_____

_____

↓

(Second subsection)

Sequence 1:

NARRATOR: _____

_____

_____

_____

_____

_____

Sequence 2:

NARRATOR: _____
_____
_____
_____
_____
_____

Sequence 3:

NARRATOR: _____
_____
_____

Transition into third subsection — NARRATOR: _____

(Third subsection)

Sequence 1:

NARRATOR: _____

_____

_____

_____

_____

_____

Sequence 2:

NARRATOR: _____
_____
_____
_____
_____
_____

Sequence 3:

NARRATOR: _____
_____
_____
_____
_____

c | Conclusion:

NARRATOR: _____

_____

_____

_____

_____

_____

DISCUSSION: When you have completed your worksheet, exchange it with one of your group members. If further elaboration on your narrator's comments is necessary, give it. If any questions arise, answer them. Generally evaluate these movie mockups (or "storyboards" in filmmakers' terminology) just as you did the articles in the last exercise.

[If you took the alternative approach suggested (filling in numbers instead of pasting in pictures), read your completed continuity aloud to your group or class and ask for evaluation.]

EXERCISE B

Prepare a brief *story* film by combining the still pictures in group B (Figure 7-7, page 179). Again, each picture is to represent a shot and each connected group of pictures a sequence. Provide a running explanation of your story as it develops.

WORKSHEET
FOR GROUP B

A | Introductory sequence (a teaser or first act):

Explanation: _____ __

_____

_____

_____

_____

_____

B Sequence 1:

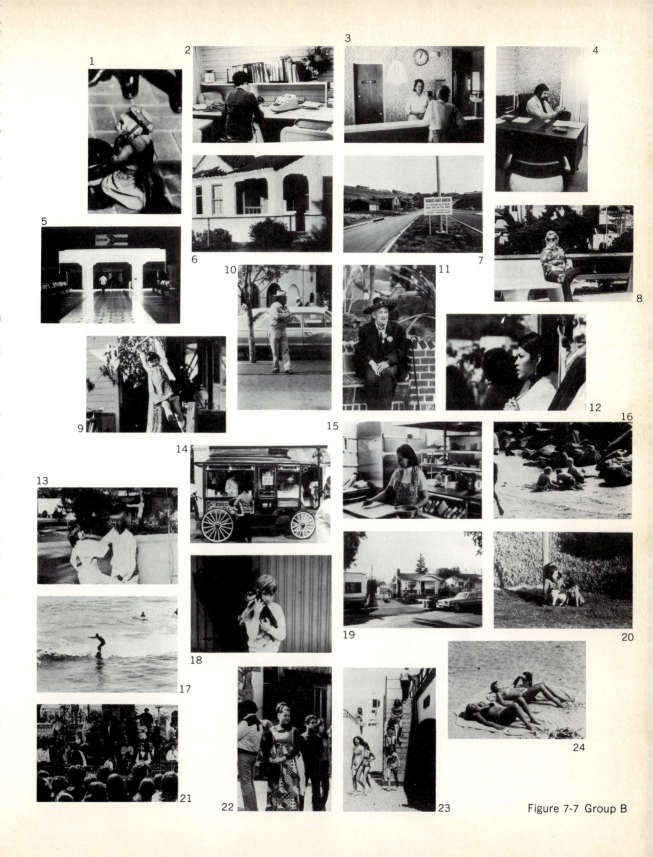

Figure 7-7 Group B

Explanation: _____

_____

_____

_____

_____

_____

Sequence 2:

B

Explanation: _____

_____

_____

_____

_____

_____

Sequence 3:

Explanation: _____

_____

_____

_____

c | Conclusion (a resolution of the story's main conflict):

Explanation: _____

_____

_____

_____

_____

_____

DISCUSSION: When you have completed your worksheet, exchange it with one of your group members. If any questions about your story arise, answer them—fill in the gaps. Generally evaluate these story films as you have evaluated the article and the documentary film in the previous exercises. Be sure to consider the effectiveness of each *as a story.* Basically, is it original and interesting? Does it grab you?

EXERCISE C

Take *either* your documentary film A or your story film B and translate *all* of it into writing—that is, into an article or a short story. Make the reader see everything as vividly as if he were looking at the pictures themselves.

[Alternative Assignment: Make an original movie with 8- or Super-8-millimeter equipment. Follow the basic format we have been discussing (the ABC breakdown). Provide some commentary to be narrated during the screening of your film. A multitude of books and brochures explaining the mechanics of home movie making are available in libraries, bookstores, and camera shops. Your instructor may be able to furnish you with film and other supplies as part of his department's materials budget. For additional fundamentals, review Chapter 6. The screening and evaluation of this film should be a classroom project.]

PART 2

chapter 8

THE GENERAL
AND THE SPECIFIC

The underlying philosophy of each chapter thus far has been that learning to write is an organic process. For this reason, *directions* on how to write have been deemed more important than an *analysis* of the principles that govern writing.

In this chapter, however, we have temporarily placed this philosophy in abeyance in order to step back, so to speak, and analyze the mechanics of what is probably the single most important principle of writing: the use of the general and the specific. It is so important, in fact, that a clear understanding and an expert use of the general and the specific should be two of the major goals of all writing classes.

There are three concepts that you must understand before you can proceed to an explanation of the general and the specific. They are *description, interpretation,* and *speculation.* These concepts are particularly indispensible if you are to understand the functions of the specific and general and the effects of their use.

TO DESCRIBE, INTERPRET, AND SPECULATE

To describe is to reproduce with words an exact image or replica of what you have seen or imagined with *no* concern for what it might mean or signify.

To interpret, on the other hand, is to define, analyze, or explain the significance of what you have observed—to pass judgment on it. The fact that you are interpreting can be obvious, or on the other hand can be expressed in such a way that it becomes evident only upon close observation. For example, the word *odd* in the phrase "the odd girl" is a judgment of that girl, hence an interpretation; however, you are not conscious that it is an interpretation unless you pause to think about it.

EXERCISE

In the parentheses preceding each sentence at the top of the following page, indicate whether that sentence is a *description* D, an *interpretation* I, or a *combination of both* DI.

1. (   ) Five young boys are standing in a group.
2. (   ) Four young boys standing in a group are enjoying themselves.
3. (   ) The girl does not want to go.
4. (   ) The man continually stares at the clock.
5. (   ) The young girl, who seems to have little in common with her peers, is sitting
         by herself.
6. (   ) Girls usually like him because he is friendly.

To speculate is to read more meaning into something than is defensibly there.
For example, if you received the simple message "The boy is afraid" and you had no
other knowledge about the situation than this, you could do either of two things.
You could be satisfied with the message as you received it, or you could *guess* at its
significance. If you did the latter, without further information, you have speculated
—that is, guessed.

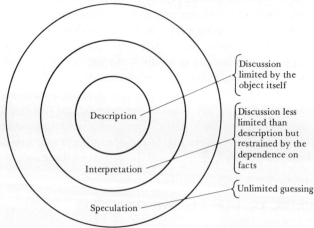

Figure 8-1

The circles in Figure 8-1 represent the potential development of a subject through
description, interpretation, and speculation. The smaller the circle, the more limited is the potential development.

The following paragraphs, written by a student, are examples of description,
interpretation, speculation, and a combination of the three. They were the student's
response to this assignment: Choose a photograph of a male or female. *Describe*
him (her), *interpret* what you see in him (her), and *speculate* upon his (her) fate.
Finally, *combine your description, interpretation, and speculation* in a short story. Figure 8-2 is the photograph the student chose.

Description

The close-up photo of Christina Gruhmann shows a young woman, sim-

Figure 8-2 *(Harlan Hoffman)*

ply dressed, leaning against a statue and gazing to her right. She wears large looped earrings, and her styled coiffure falls in loose curls across her back. Her eyes are embedded in dark, heavy makeup, and her eyebrows are shaped so that they curve downward toward her nose. Her face is angular, her cheekbones high, her chin strong, her lips sculptured full with light lipstick, and her complexion unblemished.

Interpretation

Christina Gruhmann is definitely a classic beauty. Her dark eyes and sad lips give her an air of crushing despair, yet in the deep pools of her dark eyes, one senses mystery and intrigue. From her coiffure, which is set in a classic style with soft curls falling over her unblemished, thin, bare shoulders, one can distinguish a proud woman of elegance and glamour. In the photo provided, she appears contemplative as she gazes pensively into idle space.

Speculation

Dateline: Washington, D.C.—Christina Gruhmann, alias Christine Trent, entered a federal court in Washington, D.C., on the morning of April 8, 1948. She was on trial for her life; the charge was conspiracy with Nazi Germany against the United States.

She was born on May 31, 1926, and lived in Potsdam, Germany, with her mother and a brother who died at an early age in a fire.

At the age of seventeen and after the death of her mother, she joined the National Socialist German Workers party.

After two years of training, Christina became a spy in the United States. During this time she killed the head of United States intelligence in Washington, D.C., for which she was brought to trial and condemned to death.

Combination of Description, Interpretation, and Speculation

Dateline: Washington, D.C.—Christina Gruhmann, alias Christine Trent, entered a federal court in Washington, D.C., on the morning of April 8, 1948. She was on trial for her life; the charge was conspiracy with Nazi Germany against the United States.

Born May 31, 1926, Christina grew up in Potsdam, Germany, with her mother. She had a brother, but he died in a fire in 1932. Christina, age six at the time, was spared on that fearful night. James Gruhmann, age ten, had gone into the kitchen to get a glass of water for his sister. He accidentally tipped a candle on the table in the humble living room on that Christmas Eve. When he returned from the kitchen with the water, he was encompassed by flames and perished. Christina was swept out the back door by her mother. When she reached the safety of the outdoors, she was thrust at some American tourists nearby who were watching the fire. Her mother ran to the neighboring house to contact the fire department. In the meantime the tourists put Christina in a hotel down the street where she was kept until the fire was extinguished. She had tried to tell the men about her brother but was ignored and was assumed to be nothing more than a hysterical child. As a consequence she had, since that day, held a deep hatred for the "materialistic and unfeeling American," interested only in himself. She blamed these Americans and herself for the death of her brother.

A few years later her mother died, and all alone in the world, she joined the National Socialist German Workers party at the age of seventeen. Her elegant beauty and hauntingly calm composure made her the perfect candidate as a spy for the Nazi party.

After two years of training, she was prepared to visit the United States of America under the name of Christine Trent, heiress, born in Baltimore, Maryland.

Her job, as a spy, was to seek out all the information possible about United States involvement in World War II. She was introduced to many important diplomats and men of vital value to the United States government. She seduced these men with her tempting and mysterious eyes until she learned what she wanted. It was noted by most of her "subjects" that she seldom smiled. She seemed always to be preoccupied with some sort of sadness. Even during lovemaking she seemed distant and cold.

On November 6, 1947, Christine Trent shot and killed John David Blake, head of United States intelligence in Washington, D.C., and burned down the hotel in which he was later found. She was seen leaving his room about 8:30 P.M., and the Golden Star Hotel was burned to the ground by 9:30 P.M. the same night.

After three weeks of running, she was found in a park leaning against a cold white statue among the shrubs and staring at the empty ground. On July 21, 1948, Christina Gruhmann was sentenced to death row on a charge of assassination and plotting against the United States.

As her sentence was passed, Christina turned to the people in the room and in a low and somber voice said, "Thank you for not sparing my life. It is truly a relief to leave a world of hatred, war, and loneliness. Yet, in the end, America will perish in her own blood. A country so concerned with material things and selfish motives will finally fall. I am only sorry that I will not be present to see *you* burn!"

EXERCISE

Look at Figures 8-3 and 8-4. Then do the following exercises on a separate sheet of paper.

1. *Describe* the characters in Figures 8-3 and 8-4.

2. *Interpret* the characters in Figures 8-3 and 8-4.

Figure 8-3   Figure 8-4

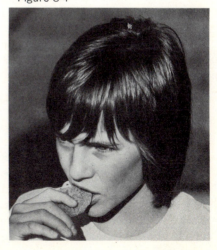

Figure 8-5 *(Omikron)*

Figure 8-6 *(Omikron)*

3. Now look at Figures 8-5 and 8-6. Assume that each character in Figures 8-3 and 8-4 is looking at each scene depicted in Figures 8-5 and 8-6. Now *speculate* upon the reaction of each girl to this experience. Write this speculation either in the first or second person. Since each has a distinctive personality, the reader should be able to distinguish which is being written about without being told explicitly.

DISCUSSION: Read your paragraphs to the members of your group, who should comment on your writing. If time permits, each group should select the best paper and have it read to the entire class.

THE GENERAL

In Chapter 6, a generalization was likened to the long shot of a camera. This analogy is based on the observation that the greater your distance from the object viewed (the focal point), the better you can see its relationship to the things around it. This phenomenon was also basic to the discussion of setting as sign in the first section (pages 32–33) and was exemplified by Figures 1-16 and 1-12.

A generalization might be defined further as a broad view which shows the relationships between the data observed by abstracting the information into one coherent statement of opinion, purpose, or organization.

Examples:
Following is a list of data that will be abstracted into three general statements expressing opinion, purpose, and organization.

planes	Communists
ships	United States
troops	tanks
South Korea	1950s

1. General statement expressing opinion:
   The United States had every right to poise its forces against the invasion of South Korea by the Communists.

2. General statement expressing purpose:
   In the early 1950s, the United States marshalled its forces to stop a Communist invasion of South Korea.

3. General statement expressing organization:
   In the Korean War, the United States coordinated the forces of the Navy, Air Force, and Army.

A general statement is an indispensible tool for indicating the overall direction of a discussion or essay or the point which will be made. You must be cautious, however, that you use generalizations only when they are needed and thereby avoid their overuse. In all media of communication, extreme or overused generalizations result in works that are impersonal or vague or analytical or uninteresting or a combination of these.

THE SPECIFIC

In Chapter 6, a specific was likened to the close-up shot of a camera. Essentially, the focal point is pure data until later qualified. At its extreme, a specific is simply a *concrete noun,* the most objective component of the language. If a generalization may be likened to a map that shows the relative location of cities, a specific may be likened to the cities themselves. You have overused specifics if your writing becomes befuddled by detail and you fail to make a point.

General and Specific Are Relative Terms

General and *specific* are relative terms and cannot be understood except in a comparative sense; hence, there are no absolute rules that can be taught governing their use. As a writer then, if you are to master the use of the specific and general, you

Increasingly specific ← → Increasingly general

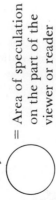
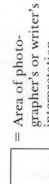
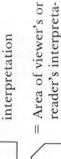

(a) (b) (c) (d) (e)

Key

= Area of speculation on the part of the viewer or reader

= Area of photographer's or writer's interpretation

= Area of viewer's or reader's interpretation

Figure 8-7

Sentences Roughly Equivalent In Specificity or Generality To The Diagrams Above.

(a) An apple is.

(b) This man is my father.

(c) Many automobile drivers passing my house are concerned only with speed.

(d) Large institutions with their politically motivated actions are a curse to this nation because of their insensitivity to change and need.

(e) Life is the most exciting thing in the universe.

Figure 8-12

Figure 8-11

Figure 8-10

Figure 8-9

Figure 8-8

must: (1) learn "to sense" the need for the specific and general through direction and example and (2) understand the mechanics of the response they effect from the reader. Chapter 6 satisfies the first requirement; the remainder of this chapter satisfies the second.

THE COMMUNICATION SPECTRUM

When something becomes hotter, it becomes less cold; when something becomes colder, it becomes less hot. The general and specific affect each other similarly. For this reason it is useful to view them as opposite ends of a spectrum.

The "spectrum" shown in Figure 8-7 has been constructed to illustrate the mechanics necessary to understand a message's relative generality or specificity. We have used photographs because their analogy to writing for our particular purpose here is so close.

At the top of the spectrum you will see a double-edged arrow that moves to the right and left from center. To the right is the direction of increased generality (abstraction); to the left is the direction of increased specificity (concreteness).

Next, you will note a series of five diagrams (*a* through *e*). These are graphic illustrations of the functions that the communicator and receiver of a message must perform relative to generality or specificity before that message can be communicated and understood. Each diagram represents the mechanics necessary for the communication and understanding of the message embodied in the picture or in the sentence directly above the picture. After checking the key for the meanings of the symbols, you will find, for example, that each diagram graphically indicates the roles that the photographer and viewer or the writer and reader must perform so that communication can occur.

In order to waylay useless argumentation, we will assume that the pictures (Figures 8-8 through 8-11) have been taken by the same photographer, that the viewer has no previous knowledge of the character and setting portrayed, and that the photgrapher was attempting to communicate a direct rather than a symbolic message.

No form of communication is distraction-free, be it a book, a record, a movie, or whatever. In a movie, for example, we can easily be distracted from the main line of communication by an attractive character, a setting we recognize, or an unusual car. When viewing and analyzing pictures we can fall into the same distractions by mistaking an insignificant part of the picture for the focal point and attempting to place the point of distraction in its proper perspective.

Below you will encounter a series of problems to solve. They have been designed to help you understand the communication spectrum we have illustrated. *It is imperative that you solve all the problems before you consult the "Introspection" sections.*

Figure 8-8

Discussion of Figure 8-8

1. As much as possible, determine the message that the photographer is trying to convey in Figure 8-8. Is the message you receive more than, "The car exists"? If so, is the message you assume you received beyond the factual meaning of the photograph itself? Have you made the message a product of your interpretation or speculation rather than the message of the photographer?

2. If the photographer had wanted to convey the message, "With this car you will develop many friends," was his attempt at communication successful? If so, why? If not, why?

3. After answering the questions above, can you conclude that a message that is overly specific naturally leads to speculation on the part of the receiver?

4. A concept is a mental image of something that you personally associate with some other things. For example, many of us associate the concept of "mother" with someone who shows tenderness, love, and care. What is your concept of the car above? If you found that your concept differed from that of the photographer after you had assumed them to be similar, would your concept have been a product of speculation? Is speculation communication?

INTROSPECTION: You probably found the potential for the interpretation of Figure 8-8 quite narrow and restrictive. You probably also found that in an attempt to expand the photograph's meaning you were tempted to add information of your own. If you did, you speculated. This means that the photographer through his photograph did not communicate his ideas to you but succeeded only in stimulating your own ideas.

It should be noted that the focal point of this picture is unmistakably clear. The fact that it has such a limited focal point leads the viewer to speculate. Speculation in this case might be compared to stepping back from a limited scene to view it in a larger context. For example, suppose you were involved in a freeway accident that involved fifty cars. From your limited vantage point you would be unable to assess the extent of the accident or even its ultimate cause. However, if you were airlifted away from the scene, the higher you rose the more you would be able to determine how the accident began and, as more cars became involved, how it became more devastating. Your perspective would be changing. In your original position you were only able to speculate upon the remote cause of the accident. As you were lifted farther away from your limited perspective, the context of your perspective was enlarged, and your ability to interpret became greater. Because your view of Figure 8-8 was so limited, you were forced to speculate to determine a message. If the photographer had included a larger context, you could have speculated less and interpreted more.

In writing, as your perspective becomes more general, it becomes more analytical and appears less emotional, just as your immediate involvement with the accident lessened the farther away from it you went.

At times you want a general perspective in your writing; however, if you view your subject too generally (from too great a distance), you may lose sight of the original images (specifics) that prompted the generalization. This often makes writing too impersonal.

Much like the overly general, the overly specific becomes very impersonal, although for different reasons. The generalization becomes impersonal because its focus is too broad; the overly specific becomes impersonal because it is too concrete and objective. Scientific and other analytical reports often appear impersonal because they combine both extremes. This is why much technical material is usually enjoyable only to the few who can either supply equivalents or broaden the context by speculating upon the possible ramifications of the facts.

Figure 8-9 *(Natasha Snyder — Omikron)*

Discussion of Figure 8-9

1.   As much as possible, *interpret* the message that the photographer is attempting to convey in Figure 8-9. Is it more or less difficult to interpret than Figure 8-8? Give reasons for your answer.

2. Assume the photographer wanted to say, "The woman is thinking." How close to this meaning was your interpretation? Did the picture invite speculation? If it did, did the photographer communicate clearly?

3. Assume that the photographer wanted to convey the message, "This woman is sad because she has just lost her husband." If you had arrived at this meaning from the picture alone, would you have been speculating or interpreting? If the above message had indeed been what the photographer wanted to communicate, was he successful?

4. Does this photograph offer you, the viewer, more information on which to base your interpretation than did Figure 8-8? If it does, what is this information?

5. Is the subject of Figure 8-9 less objective than that of Figure 8-8? If the answer is yes, does this mean that the photographer has become more interpretive?

6. The photographer has given us more context in this picture than in Figure 8-8. What is this context? Does the context help to make the picture more emotionally appealing?

7. Diagrams *a* and *b* in Figure 8-7 represent the mechanics that come to play on the part of the photographer and viewer of Figures 8-8 and 8-9, respectively. Can you explain them?

INTROSPECTION: This photograph is less concrete and objective than Figure 8-8 and, hence, invites less speculation on the part of the viewer. The photographer has developed his subject more fully by placing her in a context (her clothes, her facial expression, and her setting). That gives you, the viewer, further information by which you can develop an impression and form your interpretation. The varied interpretations that have been developed range from "despairing" to "thinking of a grocery list," however, and they indicate that the context is not developed sufficiently to communicate clearly. This photograph necessitates speculation on the part of the viewer, although not quite so much as did the previous photograph.

The focal point of this photograph, the woman, is very apparent; however, it is not quite as restricted as the focal point of Figure 8-8.

The sentence-equivalent of Figure 8-9 is, "This woman is my mother." Like its photograph-equivalent, its meaning is unsatisfying to most people because it is so limited. Again, unless you speculate, your interpretation remains descriptive, that is, limited.

Discussion of Figure 8-10

1. Look at Figure 8-10 only briefly and summarize your immediate interpretation in a sentence. Now look at it more closely. Do the details of the photograph support your superficial interpretation?

Figure 8-10 *(Harlan Hoffman)*

2. Was the message easier to interpret than the messages of Figures 8-8 and 8-9? If so, was this due to a greater development of context than was noted in the previous pictures? Did you have to speculate as much as you did for the previous pictures and their sentence-equivalents?

3. As a viewer, are you more easily interested in or involved with this particular picture than you were with the previous ones?

4. Is there a clear message in this picture? If so, does it mean that the photographer has communicated well?

5. Does this picture have a clear focal point? If you have found it, block it out with a piece of paper so that only the context is visible. How does this affect the picture? Now block out the context, leaving only the focal point. Does this graphically demonstrate that the photographer has interpreted the picture for us by including a context?

INTROSPECTION: At first glance, the impression you probably received from the photograph was basically, "A young woman is walking by a young girl and by two men—one sitting on a fountain rail—who admire her."

Analyzing the photograph closely, you probably found this interpretation supported by the details in the photograph. As a result, you felt safe to conclude from the evidence that the above impression is exactly what the photographer intended to communicate. If you are wrong, then we can justifiably conclude that the photographer has communicated his idea poorly.

On the other hand, since each person who views the photograph has a unique psychological makeup and as a result sees the photograph in his own unique way, your interpretation, too, may differ in degree from that of the photographer. For example, whereas the photographer may disagree, you may consider the young woman beautiful and may include this in your interpretation. Furthermore, you may interpret the facial expressions on the part of the males as expressions of admiration and, noting a slight smile on the girl's face, may conclude that she enjoys being admired. The latter are minor interpretive differences; the basic interpretation remains that of the photographer. You noted, when analyzing the other two photographs, on the other hand, that the photographer's role of interpreter diminished as they became more specific.

In the diagram above the picture in the communication spectrum, you will note that the area indicating interpretation on the part of the photographer is quite large when compared with the same area in the previous diagrams. This is because the photographer has qualified his statement: he lets it communicate for itself and leaves little to be interpreted by the viewer.

If in your interpretation you exceeded the limitations of the data presented by the photographer (for example, making the woman a young housewife on her way to the market) then you have entered into the realm of speculation. By doing so, you have tailored your message to fit your own bias. This is not interpreting accurately; however, no sentence is ever interpreted without some taint of bias. For this reason, diagram c has allowed for speculation.

Every photograph that communicates a message clearly has a definite focal point. It follows, also, that the more obscure the focal point of a photograph is the more *interpretation* is necessary to attempt to understand the message. This is also true of sentences.

When we look at Figure 8-10, our eyes instantaneously seek out a clue or key to an understanding of the message presented. Ultimately we realize that the girl is our key and that the message depends and revolves around her. *She is our focal point.*

Figure 8-11 *(Gabriele Wunderlich)*

Discussion of Figure 8-11

1.   Assume that the message of the photographer is, "People that ride trains are very friendly." Now glance at the picture for just a second. Did this statement seem to be expressed by the picture? Now look at the picture and analyze it more closely. Does this message hold true upon closer analysis?

2.   Before going on to the next question, try to develop a message that is comprehensive enough to include all the characters. Could this message be, "Trains are pleasant places"?

3.   Does Figure 8-11 have one easily recognizable focal point? Does it have secondary focal points? What is the main focal point? What are the secondary focal points? How does the process of pinpointing a focal point show that the structure of this photograph is different from the ones viewed previously?

4.   What relevance does this statement have to Figure 8-11? "Every photograph that communicates a message clearly has an obvious focal point. It follows also that the more obscure a focal point, the more interpretation is necessary to attempt to understand the message."

5.   Is Figure 8-11 more or less impersonal than Figures 8-9 and 8-10? Why is this so?

INTROSPECTION: If you are not analytical, the message presented in a generalization can easily be accepted by you as a true statement. On the other hand, if you are analytical, the more sweeping the generalization the more easily you can find fault with it.

A generalization is a series of observations that a writer or photographer has abstracted into a single observation. They have taken the liberty to impose their own conclusions on a set of facts. A good generalization is one that is based upon a good investigation of facts, and it generally holds true. A generalization is also acceptable when it is qualified—that is, when those parts of the generalization that don't hold true are noted.

The generalization, "People that ride trains are friendly," is not totally satisfied by Figure 8-11. You note a number of people included in the photograph who have chosen an activity that does not involve them with the rest of the passengers; hence the statement is not totally supportable. If the statement had been qualified to read, "Some people who ride trains are friendly," then it would have been acceptable.

When you read a sentence such as the following, "Large institutions are a curse to this nation because they are too cumbersome to respond to social needs," you might agree; however, if you look into your experience you might disagree because you see examples to the contrary. You have interpreted this generalization; that is, you have *supplied your own equivalents* and have found that they do not all support the statement. If the writer had allowed for these exceptions his statement might have been, "Large institutions, with a few exceptions, are a curse. . . ." If he had noted the exceptions in his mind and wanted specifically to single them out, he would have said, "Large institutions, with exceptions such as _____ and _____, are a curse. . . ." In both cases, he would have been *interpreting his own statements* more precisely. It might be noted here that generalizations invite more interpretation than speculation, as indicated by Figure 8-11.

While answering question 5, you probably found that Figure 8-11 was not initially as personal as Figures 8-9 and 8-10. This is because you were interested in the abstraction of these people, not the people themselves as individuals. The sentence, "She felt relieved," is much like this photograph because the phrase, "felt relieved," is a generalization and, hence, an abstraction. The following is the same sentence developed further: "She felt relieved as she saw her father recovering from what had been thought to be a fatal injury." This sentence became more personal with the additional development.

In some cases, the unqualified statement, "She felt relieved," would suffice if the "receiver" of the message had previous knowledge of the situation or if the message was not important enough to merit the qualification. As communicators, one of the greatest skills you must develop is the ability to know when a generalization suffices and when specifics should be added either to make the generalization more concrete and defensible or more personal.

You might finally note that the focal point of a generalization is more inclusive and abstract than the focal point of a specific. You might also note that the secondary focal points in this case make the photograph less impersonal.

Figure 8-12. Ferdinand Leger, *The City*, 1919, oil on canvas, 90¾ by 11½ inches, Philadelphia Museum of Art, The A. E. Gallatin Collection.

Discussion of Figure 8-12

1. Assume that the message the artist wants to communicate in Figure 8-12 is, "A city is made of many things." Can you identify these "many things" in the painting?

2. Does this painting have a focal point? If it does, what is it? Is it more abstract than that of Figure 8-11?

3. What relevance does the following statement have to this painting? "Every photograph that communicates a message clearly has a definite focal point. It follows also that the more obscure a focal point is, the more interpretation is necessary to attempt to understand the message."

INTROSPECTION: Figure 8-12 is a concept (an abstraction) of what a city is. It attempts to say so much about the city that even the evidence has become abstract. In fact, the statement as a whole is so abstract or general that you are tempted to agree because the task of interpretation appears so mammoth. As an abstraction Figure 8-12 has lost much of its warmth and identity — this city could be any city, even more than the people in Figure 8-11 could be any people. The work is theoretical rather than representational which is why it is so cold.

In the painting's verbal equivalent, "Life is the most exciting thing in the universe," we find a statement equally general. This is why it lacks warmth.

Mentally you react to the verbal statement much like you reacted to the painting itself — feeling a horror at the mammoth task of interpretation. This is why you often assent to such a statement without really comprehending it. And this is why such vast generalizations fail to communicate — their message is so large it is incomprehensible. It is like the very high view of the freeway that we spoke of on page 196. The picture was so large and took so much territory within its scope that it made one lose sight of the importance of the specific images.

The more the generalization is broken down, the more it relates to things you recognize as part of your experience and involves you as a participant in the idea of the statement.

chapter 9

MAKING GRAMMAR WORK: HOW TO WRITE A MORE DETAILED SENTENCE

HOW WELL DO YOU WRITE?

Before reading further, write a short paragraph in the space provided. When you have finished, continue reading.

_____

_____

_____

_____

_____

_____

_____

_____

_____

    Count the number of words in each of your sentences and determine your _average_ sentence length. If your count shows an eight-to-fifteen-word average, your writing is substandard. A computerized study has shown the average sentence length of a professional writer to be twenty-four words. Certain types of specialized writing— memos, advertisements, dialogue, directions, and some business letters—successfully utilize the short sentence; however, for the most part the cumulative effect of short sentences in other types of writing is one of amateurism, superficiality, and choppiness.

EXERCISES

1.   Establish the average sentence length in each of the following articles.

ARTICLE

It has been easy to overlook the relevance of dialect difference to education; and indeed, for the best-known American dialects it poses no great problem to ignore such differences. But if the disadvantaged black has an historically different variety of English from that of the mainstream-culture white, the question remains open as to whether lack of communication is part of the racial trouble in this country. There is enough evidence of linguistic mis-understanding between the races to make us cautious about leaving any avenue of investigation unexplored.

In the Dallas Morning News for July 13, 1967, a columnist reports with not unracist glee how a Negro got himself into rather a great deal of trouble by running from some policemen who were trying to serve him with a restrain-ing order. "They's goin' to strain me" was the explanation for his attempt to escape. Because he did not have the initial unstressed syllable in his own language system, the Black English speaker read into restrain: strain. A minor matter, except that strain means "beat" in the language of the speaker —as it does on many islands in the English-speaking part of the Caribbean.*

ARTICLE

In the hierarchy of criminals, forgers and safecrackers have long enjoyed elite status because of their special skills. Now they may be topped by the computer criminal. According to Stanford Research Institute Computer Specialist Donn B. Parker, who recently completed a study of 100 crimes involving computers, the potential for illicit gain from the machines is so vast that dishonest employees and even ambitious outsiders will increasing-ly be tempted to put their knowledge to unlawful use. A handful of key-punch crooks have already thought of some ingenious ways to defraud the Brain, with varying results.†

*J. L. Dillard, "The Validity of Black English and What to Do About It," *Intellectual Digest*, December 1972, pp. 35–36. Condensed from J. L. Dillard, *Black English: Its History and Usage in the U.S.*, Random House, New York, 1972. Copyright © 1972 by J. L. Dillard.

†"Key-Punch Crooks," *Time*, December 25, 1972, p. 69. Reprinted by permission from TIME, The Weekly Newsmagazine; Copyright Time Inc.

ARTICLE

"California's public schools are headed for a happy and prosperous new year, bringing an end to the financial squeeze that has gripped education in this state for nearly a decade.

Gov. Reagan's signature—considered a certainty—is all that remains to enact a school finance-tax relief bill that will disgorge $2 billion in new state money for schools over the next three years.

The fat package will be divided about equally between new dollars to run schools and funds to slash property taxes levied by school districts.

It will give schools about $332 million more in operating funds in the first year (1973–74)—a whopping 20% jump.*

ARTICLE

The Miami Dolphins began what their players like to call "the money season" by driving 80 yards in the closing minutes Sunday to a go-ahead touchdown before their "No-Name" defense saved the victory over the Cleveland Browns.

By a 20–14 margin, the undefeated Dolphins won their 15th straight game and the right to meet the Steelers in Pittsburgh next Sunday for the AFC championship.

The Dolphins came perilously close to elimination at the hands of a Cleveland team seemingly impervious to playoff pressure or the 80,010 screaming Dol-fans in the Orange Bowl.†

2.   Establish the average length of sentences found in articles and stories you have read outside class.

DISCUSSION: Compare your information with that of other students. What conclusions can you reach from your data? Were you aware of the importance of sentence length prior to this?

Why the Long Sentence?

Ironically, the reason for lengthy sentences is to make your writing compact. A paragraph composed of short sentences tends to be wordy because so many transitional phrases are needed and because what may be expressed as a modifier in a

---

*Jack McCurdy, "State Schools Await Prosperous New Year," *Los Angeles Times,* December 10, 1972. Copyright, 1972, Los Angeles Times. Reprinted by permission.

†Leonard Shapiro, "Dolphins, Facing First Defeat, Rally to Beat Cleveland, 20–14," *Los Angeles Times,* December 25, 1972. Copyright, 1972, Los Angeles Times. Reprinted by permission.

more lengthy sentence is given the status of a complete sentence. Not every sentence, however, must be long to be effective, nor should words be added to a sentence only to make it long, for this would result in wordy and meaningless word groups. Rather, sentences of different lengths should be used for different effects: long sentences to give context; short sentences to summarize or to make or emphasize a point.

How Does One Build a Long Sentence?

The ability to write a long sentence is normally achieved by the slow process of trial and error or by the imitation of others' writings. Happily, there is a method by which one can minimize this learning period. This is simply to learn the function of the grammatical structures of the language and to utilize them in writing. This differs from the traditional grammar approach in that the latter emphasizes the *identification* of structures rather than their *utilization*.

How Much Grammar Will You Learn?

The following series of definitions and exercises are not intended to give examples of every structural possibility in the English language, but rather to present some basic elementary structural possibilities for lengthening sentences and making them more complex. In order to present these structures as simply as possible, we have attempted to streamline the rules. To do this we have minimized the exceptions and the fine points of syntax and have assumed that you have an elementary grasp of grammar.

THE SENTENCE—THE STUFF THAT ENGLISH IS MADE OF

The sentence, as described on pages 209–210, is one of the most basic elements of communication. Its function is to present an idea and show the relationship of that idea to those expressed in preceding or following sentences.

Sentences are built upon identifiable foundations or structures. Denuded of modification, these structures, although sentences by definition, are purely functional, colorless, and insipid, and without precision or "personality." They are much like the chassis of a car with a motor mounted on it—a car by definition, but hardly a replacement for a totally assembled car.

The following paragraphs dramatically exemplify the different effects achieved by a paragraph of basic sentence structures and one that uses the same structures but also develops them with modifiers.

Basic Structures:
Sagas are written. This novel is a case. We have got a genealogy. The tone continues. The most vivid are sisters and a girl.

Developed Structures:

Sagas, especially minisagas, are not easily written. This softly modulated novel of a provincial Polish rabbi's son who emigrated to cosmopolitan Warsaw and then to London just before World War I is a touching case in point. By the time young Mendel quits his one-droshky town to seek his fortune, we have got an entire family genealogy crusty with Hassidic lore and ritual. The tone of the tale spinner (with perhaps too many reverse spins into flashback) continues as Mendel joins his restless, modernist cousin working in their uncle's dreary diamond shop in London, takes up with emerging Socialists and Zionists struggling for Jewish allegiance, and falls in with liberated ladies. The most vivid of these are two radiclib Yiddish sisters and a milk-complexioned gentile girl who sorely tests his powers to resist assimilation and remain a real Jew.*

Basic sentence structures are composed of three parts of speech: *nouns, verbs,* and *adjectives. Nouns* are simply defined as words that can be pluralized (cat, cats) and changed to the possessive (cat, cat's). *Verbs* are defined as words that will fit into the pattern "love," "loves," "loved." *Adjectives* are defined as words that will fit into patterns like "loud," "louder," "loudest" or "beautiful," "more beautiful," "most beautiful."

The following are four of the most common sentence structures:

1.   Noun (N) and verb (V).

      Examples:

	N	V
(The)	apples	rotted.
	Clouds	moved.
	Girls	cry.

2.   Noun (N) and verb (V) and noun (N).

      Examples:

	N	V		N
(The)	boys	caused	(a)	fight.
(The)	children	killed	(the)	spider.
(His)	eye	caught	(the)	movement.

3.   Noun (N) and linking verb (LV) and noun (N). The verbs that commonly occur in this pattern are "am," "is," "are," "was," "were," "seem," "appear," and "look."

*"Out of the Ghetto," *Newsweek,* November 13, 1972, p. 108. Copyright Newsweek, Inc., 1972; reprinted by permission.

Examples:

	N	LV		N
(The)	table	is		metal.
	Telephones	are		instruments.
	Henry	is	(a)	cheerleader.
	Bob	looked	(the)	part.

4.   Noun (N) and linking verb (LV) and adjective (A). The verb in this pattern is always a linking verb (am, is, are, was, were, seem, appear, look, taste, feel, or grow). Linking verbs function as an equivalent sign ($=$). For example, Mary is ($=$) a girl.

Examples:

	N	LV	A
(The)	man	looks	crazy.
(The)	steak	tastes	delicious.
	Brown	is	beautiful.

The four sentence structures might be represented as follows:

N	V	
N	V	N
N	LV	N
N	LV	A

How Sentences Grow

The initial areas of development in the sentence usually occur around the basic nouns (N) and verbs (V). In the sentence N V N, for example, the verb and both nouns are the central focus around which development occurs. It may be noted that this development coincidentally introduces areas which themselves may be developed following the same rules that were used in the original development.

The elaboration which occurs around the noun becomes a part of a unit called a "noun cluster," that is, the noun and all its modifiers. When the elaboration occurs around a verb, it becomes a part of the unit called a "verb cluster," that is, the verb and all its modifiers. You will learn how to develop such clusters in the sections that follow.

MODIFIERS OF NOUNS

The first area of development will be that of the noun cluster. In the noun cluster, each noun modifier usually follows a specific order. It would be unusual to find all possible noun modifiers present in a single sentence. The noun modifiers developing the nouns in the sentence N V N would form noun clusters in the following order:

NOUN CLUSTER	VERB	NOUN CLUSTER
D A V-"ING" N PN APP V-"ING" ADJ CL V-"ED" V-"ED"	V	D A V-"ING" N PN APP V-"ING" ADJ CL V-"ED" V-"ED"

Each noun modifier will be defined individually. The adjective, designated as A in the noun cluster overviews above, will be discussed first.

Adjectives (A)

One of the main functions of an adjective (A) is to describe. In this capacity, most adjectives are used to tell how the author feels about the noun he is describing.

For the sake of simplification, the overview of the noun clusters above shows only one adjective (A), although in actuality there could be more than one, as demonstrated by the second and third examples that follow.

The usual position of an adjective is between the determiner (D) and the noun (N). Determiners are words such as "the," "a," "an," "these," "those," "her," "this," "that," "my," "several," "one," "two," "either," or "neither," which signal that a noun is coming.

Examples:

D	A	A	A	N
The	large			harbor . . .
A	silent,	dreamy		night . . .
That	loud,	egotistical,	and obnoxious	girl . . .

The adjectives that are used in the examples above clearly express the opinion of the writer.

EXERCISES

1.   Read the passage below, then fill the blanks with adjectives. Try to make them as imaginative and vivid as possible.

As he drove through the _____ countryside, the _____ man kept his _____ eyes glued to the _____ road. His thoughts dwelled upon his _____ future now that his once _____ funds were nearly depleted. His intentions had been _____, but his perseverance had been tried and defeated by the _____ misfortunes that would test any man, even one of _____ endurance. NOTE: You might compare adjectives to makeup—when used sparingly and strategically, they can do much to enhance; when used in excess, they can be too obvious and distracting.

2. Examine Figures 9-1 to 9-6 carefully and in the space provided characterize each with ten perceptive adjectives.

FIGURE 9-1   FIGURE 9-2   FIGURE 9-3

_____   _____   _____

_____   _____   _____

_____   _____   _____

_____   _____   _____

_____   _____   _____

_____   _____   _____

_____   _____   _____

_____   _____   _____

FIGURE 9-4   FIGURE 9-5   FIGURE 9-6

_____   _____   _____

_____   _____   _____

_____   _____   _____

_____   _____   _____

_____   _____   _____

Figure 9-1 (Omikron)

Figure 9-2 (Omikron)

Figure 9-3 (Gabriele Wunderlich)
Figure 9-5 (Gabriele Wunderlich)

Figure 9-4 (J. J. Valario)
Figure 9-6 (Gabriele Wunderlich)

FIGURE 9-4 (continued)   FIGURE 9-5 (continued)   FIGURE 9-6 (continued)

_____   _____   _____

_____   _____   _____

_____   _____   _____

_____   _____   _____

_____   _____   _____

3.   On a separate sheet of paper, write six short pharagraphs describing the preceding six photographs. Utilize some of the adjectives you have already chosen.

Occasionally adjectives are placed after the nouns they modify, in which case they are separated from the rest of the sentence by commas to indicate their unusual position. The reasons for placing adjectives in this position might be summarized as follows:

1.   To emphasize the adjective or adjectives placed in this position.

Examples:
Original sentence:

    A   A   A   N

The old, strict, and stubborn professor was never forgotten by his students.
Altered sentence:

    N   A A   A

The professor, old, strict, and stubborn, was never forgotten by his students.

2.   To avoid monotony and awkwardness in a series.

Examples:
Original sentence:

    A   A   A   N

The prospective, bold, and inventive candidate was a master at interviews.
Altered sentence:

    A   N   A   A

The prospective candidate, bold and inventive, was a master at interviews.

3.   To relocate an adjective which needs some further qualification. This qualification is enclosed in parentheses in the following examples.

Examples:
Original sentence:

     A   A   N

The young and renowned model established a fan club for herself.
Altered sentence:

     A   N   A

The young model, renowned (because of her eccentricities), established a fan club for herself.
Original sentence:

     A   N   A   N

Her unexplainable, radical, and reactionary personality found little favor among her peers.
Altered sentence:

     A   N   A   A

Her unexplainable personality, (ironically) radical (at times) and reactionary (at others), found little favor among her peers. (Since radical and reactionary are contradictory terms, they must be explained. For this reason they were relocated to follow the noun.)

EXERCISES

Rewrite the following sentences by placing each underlined adjective after the noun it modifies and qualifying it. Use the sentences in example 3 above as your models. Shift only the underlined adjectives.

      A   N

1.   The popular book became quite controversial.

          _____

          _____

      A   A   N

2.   The stubborn but interesting woman was liked by those who met her.

          _____

          _____

3.   His <u>inapparopriate</u> <u>remark</u> was a cause for his embarrassment among his friends.

        A   N

_____

_____

        A   N

4.   His <u>exhausted</u> <u>body</u> could go no farther.

_____

_____

Prepositional Phrases Modifying Noun (PN)

As modifiers of nouns, prepositional phrases (PN, that is, *preposition* plus *noun*) are very versatile. For this reason they are one of the most commonly used modification structures. These are some of their most important functions:

1.   To establish an environment for the noun or a particular of the noun's environment.

    Examples:

D	A	N	PN	PN
The	loud	man	in the market . . .	
The	interesting	shops	along the highway	in Laguna . . .
The	young	boy	on the bench	in the park . . .

    NOTE: Although the overview of the noun clusters on page 211 shows only one prepositional phrase (PN), in practice you will find more than one as indicated by the examples you just read.

2.   To establish a position for the noun in time.

    Examples:

D	A	N	PN
The	long	day	after the disaster . . .
Many	anxious	moments	during the trial . . .

3.   To establish an association between the noun modified and the noun introduced by the prepositional phrase.

    Examples:

D	N	PN
Her	feelings	about hippies . . .

  Complaints <u>concerning the housing</u> . . .

4. To "qualify" the noun modified.

Examples:

D	N	PN

The committee <u>for peace</u> . . .
His   expression <u>of helplessness</u> . . .

NOTE: Prepositional phrases with varied functions may be combined.

Example:

D	N	PN	PN	PN

His declaration <u>of support</u> <u>before the crowd</u> <u>during the rally</u> . . .

A preposition introducing a prepositional phrase modifying a noun might be further defined as a word that connects one noun with another and describes their relationship. For example, the relationship between the two nouns "dog" and "road" can be established by a number of prepositions such as "on" (the dog <u>on</u> the road "at" (the dog <u>at</u> the road), or "beside" (the dog <u>beside</u> the road).

Since nouns usually represent physical objects, they add or introduce a feeling of objectivity and substance to the sentence.

In the overview of noun modifiers on page 211 the prepositional phrase was designated by the abbreviation PN. It should be noted here that prepositional phrases have their own internal structure composed of their own modifying units. It might also be noted here that prepositional phrases can also modify verbs, as you will see in the section explaining verb modifiers.

Every prepositional phrase in a sentence introduces a new noun which is capable of being modified just as the original noun was. For example, the noun in the prepositional phrase "in the seat" which appears in the sentence "The unobtrusive man in the seat went unnoticed" can be modified as was the original noun "man." The modification might result in a sentence such as this:

       PN   PN

The unobtrusive man <u>in the crowded seat</u> <u>of the car</u> went unnoticed.

In this sentence, we have modified the noun "seat" with the adjective "crowded" and with the prepositional phrase "of the car." We can develop the noun "car" in the prepositional phrase "of the car" in the same way.

     PN   PN   PN

The unobtrusive man <u>in the crowded seat</u> <u>of the old and dilapidated car</u> <u>at the curb</u> went unnoticed.

Since the prepositional phrases and the adjectives added modify the original noun "seat," they are considered a part of the internal structure of the original phrase "in the seat."

The following is a partial list of prepositions:

TIME

after	behind	through
around	during	throughout
before	since	under

ENVIRONMENT

aboard	behind	into
about	below	near
above	beneath	on
across	beside	onto
against	between	over
along	beyond	round
alongside	by	throughout
amid	down	under
among	from	up
around	in	upon
at	inside	within
before		

ASSOCIATION

about	concerning	with

QUALIFICATION

for	from	of

EXERCISES

1. Develop the following sentences with the modifiers suggested. Make certain that each modifies the word indicated by the arrow if one is included. The designation indicating a prepositional phrase PN can be taken to signify a developed prepositional phrase, that is, not only the preposition and the noun but also modifiers of that noun. First read the sentence and then decide whether you want to develop the noun in *time*, create an *environment* for it, *associate* something with it, or *qualify* it. After deciding, check the list above for the prepositions that you might employ. Be sure that the prepositional phrases you add are internally well qualified.

Example:

Undeveloped sentence:

The ____(A)____ woman ____(PN)____ and ____(PN)____ attempted to find the manager ____(PN)____ .

Developed sentence:

   A   PN   PN

The sickly woman in a dress shabby with age and wear and (in) unpolished shoes

                              PN

attempted to find the manager of the department store.

a. Many ____(A)____ citizens ____(PN)____ complained about the ____(A)____ and ____(A)____ taxes ____(PN)____ .

_____

_____

b. The ____(A)____ box was open only after the ____(A)____ girl ____(PN)____ was advised to do so.

_____

_____

c. The ____(A)____ accident ____(PN)____ was a(n) ____(A)____ occurrence ____(PN)____ .

_____

_____

2. In the sentences below, develop the blanks as indicated. The brackets enclose the entire developed prepositional phrase.

Example:

Undeveloped sentence:

The ____(A)____ anticipation [____(PN)____ ____(PN)____] was clearly evident in the ____(A)____ crowd ____(PN)____ .

Developed sentence:

   A   PN   PN

The nervous anticipation of the nationally televised game between the old rivals

                                     A   PN

Notre Dame and U.S.C. was clearly evident in the <u>large</u> crowd <u>at the Colosseum</u>.

a. The account [___PN___ ___PN___] was whispered throughout the
___A___ community ___PN___ .

_____

_____

b. <u>The letter</u> [___PN___ ___PN___] told the story [___PN___
___PN___].

_____

_____

c. The parties [___PN___ ___PN___] and were considered the two
___A___ parties of the year.

_____

_____

3.   Expand the three sentences below with as many prepositional phrases as you can. Underline each prepositional phrase.

a. The women expressed hope. _____

_____

_____

b. The car stalled. _____

_____

_____

c. The night became more exasperating. _____

_____

_____

Figure 9-7

4. Imagine that you were a witness to the action depicted in Figure 9-7. On a separate sheet of paper describe what you saw to an imaginary newspaper reporter. Use as many prepositional phrases in your sentences as you can.

5. Imagine that you have recently met the characters in Figures 9-8 and 9-9. On a separate sheet of paper, by using as many prepositional phrases in your sentences as you can, describe these people to an imaginary friend. Include information on where and how you met them.

Figure 9-8   Figure 9-9

Verb-"ing" Phrases Modifying a Noun (V-"ing")

A verb-"ing" is a verb plus -ing (the verb "run" plus -ing is "running"). Generally, these phrases show the noun *acting, being,* or *existing.* They are particularly useful for describing a scene in the present that is characterized by a *great deal of action.* They can have their own modifiers or introduce their own nouns, all of which become part of the phrase.

In the examples that follow, V-"ing" modifiers are enclosed in parentheses.

Examples:

D	N	V-"ING"	V-"ING" MODIFIERS
The	laughter	echoing	(through the halls and empty rooms of the dormitory) . . .
The	tree	swinging	(wildly) . . .
The	mob	screaming throwing attacking	(obscenities), (rocks), and (the police) . . .

For the sake of simplicity, only one V-"ing" phrase was included after the noun in the overview of the noun modifiers. In practice, two or more V-"ing" phrases are often found after the noun as in example 3 above. V-"ing's" can have their own modifiers, all of which are considered part of the V-"ing" phrase. The modifiers in the following examples are enclosed in parentheses.

In addition to their position immediately after the noun, as in the previous examples, verb-"ing's" commonly appear in two other positions:

1.   Between the determiner and the noun.

Examples:

D	V-"ING"	N
The	laughing	boy . . .
The	shining	star . . .

2.   After the main verb and its modifiers for emphasis. (Note that this position is not included in the overview of noun modifiers which appears on page 211.)

Examples:

    V   V-"ING"

He was alone at last, standing (almost defiantly against the sunset).

    V   V-"ING"

He smiled at the audience, pretending (that he was not aware of their anger).

Verb-"ed" Phrases Modifying a Noun (V-"ed")

A verb-"ed" is a verb plus -ed (the verb "call" plus -ed is "called"). These phrases are used to show a relationship of the noun modified to a past action or one in the immediate past. Like V-"ing's," V-"ed's" can have their own modifiers, all of which are considered part of the V-"ed" phrase. These modifiers are enclosed in parentheses in the following examples:

Examples:

D	N	V-"ED"
The	bear	hunted (for many years) . . .
The	records	burned (by the college students although they contained harmless information) . . .
The	man	torn (by guilt), haunted (by fear), and destroyed (by shame) . . .

For the sake of simplicity only one V-"ed" phrase was included after the noun in the overview of the noun modifiers. In practice, two or more V-"ed" phrases are often found after the noun as in example 3 above.

In addition to its position immediately after the noun as in the previous examples verb-"ed's" commonly appear in two other positions:

1. Between the determiner and the noun.

   Examples:

D	V-"ED"	N
The	deserted	street . . .
The	hammered	nail . . .

2. After the main verb.

   Examples:

   D   A   N   V   V-"ED"

   The clear stream flowed down the isolated canyon, unspoiled (by man).

   N   V   V-"ED"

   He left the country, discouraged (by riots and political corruption).

EXERCISES

Fill the blanks with the appropriate structure. The designation *V-"ed"* or *V-"ing"* can also designate a developed phrase. The arrows indicate the words to be modified.

Example:

Undeveloped:

The _____(A)_____ citizen ____(V-"ED")____ is a _____(A)_____ phenomenon
_____(PN)_____ _____(PN)_____ .

Developed:

The ordinary citizen exasperated by the ineptitude of government and the in-ability to do anything about it is a common phenomenon in the large cities of the United States.

1. The _____(A)_____ novel ____(V-"ED")____ and ____(V-"ED")____ was finally confis-cated by the _____(A)_____ teacher ____(PN)____ .

_____

_____

_____

2. The airplane ____(V-"ING")____ and ____(V-"ING")____ crashed near the crowd, ____(V-"ING")____ .

_____

_____

_____

3. The _____(A)_____ remarks ____(PN)____ ____(V-"ING")____ were the cause of her _____(A)_____ departure.

_____

_____

_____

4. The place ____(V-"ED")____ was a perfect place for a party.

_____

_____

_____

5. His heart ____(V-"ING")____ , the young man approached the police officer ____(V-"ING")____ .

_____

_____

_____

Adjective Clauses Modifying A Noun (Adj Cl)

Adjective clauses have much the same function as verb-"ing" and verb-"ed" phrases, and in many cases they might even be used in place of each other. For example, the underlined clause in the sentence "The students who are screaming obscenities are ill-bred" may be rewritten as a verb-"ing" phrase "screaming obscenities." And in the sentence "The civil rights march which was organized by students was a success" the clause underlined may be rewritten as a verb-"ed" phrase: "The civil rights march organized by students was a success." In both cases above, it would be better to use the verb phrase because it is less wordy. Adjective clauses are usually introduced by the connectors "which," "who," "whose," "that," and "whom." In a series of clauses, only the first is usually introduced by a connector, unless the clauses are long, and a connector is needed to clarify the series. For the sake of clarity, only one adjective clause (Adj Cl) was included after the noun in the overview of noun modifiers on page 211. In practice and very often in good writing, two or more adjective clauses are found after the noun as in example 3 below.

Adjective Clauses Whose Verbs Are in the Present Tense.   As do verb-"ing" phrases, these clauses most frequently describe the noun modified as acting, being, or existing.

Examples:

D	N	ADJ CL
The	criticism	which we are giving . . .
All	people	who live as animals . . .
	Money	that buys food,
		(that) provides clothing, and
		(that) brings relief to the poor of America . . .

Adjective Clauses Whose Verbs Are in the Past Tense.   These clauses show the relationship of the noun modified to a past action or one in the immediate past.

Examples:

D	N	ADJ CL
The	remarks	which came from the audience . . .
The	plane	which had been buffeted by winds and (which) was

considered lucky to have continued flying . . .

The   children   who had seen the accident and (who) had attempted to summon help . . .

EXERCISES

Develop the sentences below with the modifiers suggested. Be certain that they modify the word indicated by the arrow if one is included.

1.   Seven years _____(PN)_____ _____(ADJ CL)_____ were years spent achieving little _____(ADJ CL)_____.

_____

_____

_____

_____

2.   The _____(A)_____ bus _____(ADJ CL)_____ would daily wind its way through the town _____(PN)_____ _____(V-"ED")_____.

_____

_____

_____

_____

3.   _____(A)_____ words from the crowd _____(ADJ CL)_____ were hurled at the demonstrators _____(V-"ING")_____.

_____

_____

_____

_____

4. I always consider novels ____(ADJ CL)____, ____(ADJ CL)____, and ____(ADJ CL)____ as the most interesting.

    _____

    _____

    _____

    _____

5. The trip ____(ADJ CL)____ took her into areas ____(ADJ CL)____.

    _____

    _____

    _____

    _____

6. Each boy ____(V-"ING")____ was satisfied with the ____(A)____ decision ____(ADJ CL)____.

    _____

    _____

    _____

    _____

Appositions Qualifying Proper and Common Nouns (App)

Proper nouns are names of people, things, places, or institutions. The extent to which a proper noun may be qualified is more limited than that of a common noun. For this reason a *common noun (an apposition) denoting the same person or thing* is often introduced after the proper noun because this common noun can be qualified and as a result indirectly modify the proper noun. Common nouns may also be qualified by appositions (App). The modifiers of the apposition are enclosed in parentheses in the following examples. These modifiers are considered part of the apposition.

Examples:
Proper noun:

N   APP

<u>Jim,</u>   a (young) man (embittered because of many misfortunes) . . .
<u>Lockheed,</u>   a corporation (with a history of misfortunes) . . .

Common noun:

D   N   APP

The   <u>sailor,</u>   a (bright-eyed) kid (from a small farm in Nebraska), . . .

EXERCISES

Rewrite the following sentences and fill in the appositions and their modifiers where they are called for. Attempt to make the apposition extensive.

1.   Mr. Ramires, _____(APP)_____, was an invaluable help to us.

    _____

    _____

2.   We made a promise never to visit the house, _____(APP)_____.

    _____

    _____

3.   The old gun, _____(APP)_____, was the only memento the man had to leave to his son.

    _____

    It may have become evident to you that noun modifiers have two primary functions: (1) to describe or (2) to add physical substance to a sentence. Of all the noun modifiers, none is so common as the prepositional phrase. Adjectives are used sparingly and strategically; adjective clauses are used occasionally; verb-"ing's" and verb-"ed's" are popular especially as modifiers before the noun.

EXERCISES

The following are excerpts taken from magazines and newspapers. Read them carefully and note how their authors have used noun modifiers.

1.   The first excerpt, taken from *Newsweek,* is about Joyce Carol Oates, a well-known American author. In this particular excerpt you are asked to note adjectives (underlined) and verb-"ing's" (in parentheses).

She is a tall, pale young woman with enormous eyes and a timid, little-girl voice who rather plaintively assures interviewers, "I'm not that interesting." If you met her at a literary party and failed to catch her name, it might be hard to imagine her (reading), much less (writing), the (unflinching) fiction that has made Joyce Carol Oates perhaps the most significant novelist to have emerged in the United States in the last decade.

At 34, her (sweeping) vision of America as a delusive wonderland of (colliding) forces, where love as often as hate leads to violence, has established Miss Oates as a major—and controversial—figure in American writing. Her frailness is deceptive. In less than ten years she has published five powerfully (disquieting) novels, *With (Shuddering) Fall, A Garden of Earthly Delights, Expensive People, Them* for which she won the *National* Book Award in 1970, and *Wonderland.**

2. The second excerpt, from the *Intellectual Digest,* concerns amnesty. You are asked to note the prepositional phrases which have been underlined.

The question of amnesty and/or pardon to draft evaders and deserters is not really a legal or constitutional question. There is no doubt about the constitutional right of the president to grant pardon and to proclaim amnesty; nor is there any about the congressional right to enact amnesty. Traditionally, it is the executive that has taken the initiative in granting amnesty, but recent executives have displayed less interest in amnesty than was customary in the nineteenth century. Thus, there was no amnesty after the Korean War, and there has been none so far in this war. The argument for amnesty is threefold: historical, ethical and practical. It is to the interesting question of experience, the illuminating question of expediency and the elevated question of moral obligation that we should address ourselves.†

3. The third excerpt, from the *Los Angeles Times,* concerns the morale of policemen. You are asked to note the adjective clauses (in parentheses) and prepositional phrases (underlined).

Most people (who work for a living) head for their jobs with morale at rock bottom. It doesn't go up until the end of their eight hours.

That's because most jobs are lousy. With all the talk about the work ethic, the majority of people (who work for a living) aren't wild about what they do. They do it because they have to make a living. If Johnson asked the

---

*"Joyce Carol Oates: Love and Violence," *Newsweek,* December 11, 1972, p. 72. Copyright Newsweek, Inc., 1972; reprinted by permission.

†Henry Steele Commager, "Amnesty," *Intellectual Digest,* December 1972, p. 106.

people on the assembly lines, the punch presses, the open hearths, the loading platforms, the stock rooms, the freight elevators, the mail rooms, the boiler rooms, how their morale is, most would say: "Are you nuts?"

Or stop in a coffee shop [where the salesmen are getting together with their district manager before going off to peddle a product (they don't care about)] and ask them why their stomachs are knotted. Salesmen have to give themselves rah-rah talks about positive thinking. If they don't they might head for a bar instead of a customer.

Get on a commuter train, and see how many beaming, smiling faces there are, as they approach another shift of making the rent. It's not the weather (that gives them that weary look so early in the day.)

And these are people with jobs. For a real look at low morale, try the waiting rooms of the employment agencies, or some of the men (who are cut from skilled jobs after they turn 40).*

4.   On a separate sheet of paper describe Figure 9-10 and Figure 9-11 by using as many prepositional phrases in your sentences as you can.

5.   Write a paragraph which incorporates descriptions of Figures 9-12 to 9-15. In this paragraph try to fill your sentences with the modifying structures that you have learned thus far.

MODIFIERS OF VERBS

The following is a brief survey of some of the modifiers of verbs and their functions.

Prepositional Phrases Modifying Verbs (PN)

We have seen that prepositional phrases modify nouns; now we will see how they modify verbs. In both cases the effect of their use is to add context to the sentence by introducing nouns.

Prepositional phrases modifying verbs indicate among other things: (1) the place of the action, (2) the time of the action, (3) the manner of the action, (4) the reason for the action, or (5) the receiver of the action. (See page 218 for a list of prepositions.)

Examples:

D	N	V	PN
The	phantom	appeared	at six o'clock. (time)
	We	walked	along the water. (place)

---

*Mike Royko, "Policemen and the Myth of the Work Ethic," *Los Angeles Times,* December 10, 1972. Reprinted with permission from the Chicago Daily News.

Figure 9-10 *(Omikron)*

Figure 9-11

Figure 9-12 *(Gabriele Wunderlich)*

Figure 9-13 *(Harlan Hoffman)*

Figure 9-14

Figure 9-15 *(Harlan Hoffman)*

The	woman	behaved	like a kid. (manner)
	He	gave it	to him. (receiver)
	She	came	for the magazine. (reason)

Verb-"ing" and verb-"ed" verbs are considered verbs and as such can be modified by prepositional phrases as well as by those verb modifiers yet to be defined.

Example:

```
         ┌──────────────────┐
         ▼                  ┐
   N   V-"ING"  PN          PN
```

The young child running from his father to his mother tripped on a picnic
        N   V-"ED"

```
         ┌────────┐
   N   V-"ED"     ┐
         ▼      PN         PN
         └────────────────┐
                          ▼
```

basket placed there by a group of hippies.

EXERCISES

1. Read the following passage and note how the author has developed his idea using a great number of prepositional phrases. We have underlined the prepositional phrases modifying nouns and enclosed those modifying verbs in parentheses. Often, a prepositional phrase modifies another prepositional phrase and thereby is in reality a part of it; however, to simplify matters we have separated them.

> The Heartbreak Kid is billed as a collaboration between two major comic talents, screenwriter-playwright Neil Simon and director Elaine May. It is, (in fact), a pitched battle for supremacy between Simon's gentle, essentially realistic comedy of the commonplace and Ms. May's acerbic, annihilating and sophisticated satire of middle-class American folkways. (In the end), May obliterates Simon (in a clearly Pyrrhic victory), for her fascinating, brilliantly complex film itself lies (in disarray).
>   Elaine May operates (through psychological urgencies), (through hyperbole), (by inflating ordinary fallibilities) (into grotesque and often hilarious parodies) of human behavior. Simon, (on the other hand), is a consummate craftsman in a traditionally realistic mode, carefully placing the underpinnings of objective probability (beneath every comic scene). Mike Nichols was able to collaborate (with this approach), to embellish it (with directorial invention). But his onetime partner, Ms. May, is after something a good deal more fierce and devastating.*

*"Love on the Lam," Newsweek, December 25, 1972, p. 76. Copyright Newsweek, Inc., 1972; reprinted by permission.

2. Using as many prepositional phrases as you can, write a paragraph on a separate piece of paper. Describe something which might be considered a piece of junk but which you keep for sentimental reasons. You might include a description of how you obtained it and why it has such value to you.

Adverbial Clauses Modifying Verbs (Adv Cl)

Adverbial clauses are sentences like those described on pages 208–210. They are placed within another sentence by a process called subordination and are made dependent on that sentence. This process is simply the addition of one of the many connectors mentioned below, which reduces the status of the subordinated sentence to that of a learning sentence (page 194) or modifier. This connector is the "umbilical cord" connecting the subordinated sentence to the "mother" sentence. The function of the adverbial clause is primarily to express the following: time, condition, reason, place, and concession.

Time. When the adverbial clause expresses *time,* it is introduced by such connectors as "after," "as," "as soon as," "before," "since," "when," "whenever," "while," or "until." An adverbial clause expressing time clarifies the relative time relationship between itself and the verb that it modifies.

Example:

ADV CL   N   V   V

While the shopkeeper was not looking, the clever boy would steal candy and

V   ADV CL

would leave before anyone could catch him.

NOTE: Prepositional phrases and adverbial clauses modifying the main verb can go either before the subject of the sentence or after the main verb:

Examples:

PN   N   V   N

After he threw it, the child chased the ball.

N   V   N   PN

The child chased the ball after he threw it.

This is fortunate because it enables the writer to separate: (1) two adverbial clauses that modify the same verb, or (2) an adverbial clause or a prepositional phrase, and an adverbial or adjective clause. In each case a potentially clumsy or ambiguous situation is avoided.

Examples:

ADV CL

Although they were given little chance of finding the treasure, the two men

V   N   ADJ CL

began their trip, which promised to take them to the many unexplored areas of the world.

ADV CL   V   ADV CL

After the car passed, the dog barked until someone could quiet him.

ADV CL   V   PN

Although it was unexpected, the first frost arrived in early September.

EXCEPTION: Adverbial clauses which modify the same verb and are introduced by the same connector should not be separated.

Example:

V   ADV CL

The boy's mother called him as soon as he locked the gate,

                                      put his bike away, and

                                      brushed his pants off.

Condition.   When the adverbial clause expresses *condition,* it is introduced by such connectors as "if," "unless," and "until." An adverbial clause expressing condition indicates the conditions in the past, present, or future necessary before the "meaning" or "action" expressed by the verb can be considered "completed."

Examples:

ADV CL   V   V   ADV CL

If you loved me, you would understand that I cannot leave until my work is done.

V-"ING"   ADV CL

His mind, running wild until it found the right idea, always produced something creative.

Reason.   When the adverbial clause expresses *reason,* it is introduced by such connectors as "since," "because," and, "in order that." An adverbial clause expressing reason indicates the cause or reason for the action expressed by the verb.

Examples:

```
┌─────────────────────────────────┐
ADV CL                            V
```

Since he refused to express his objection, the vote <u>was passed</u> unanimously.

```
  ┌──────────────┐
  V          ADV CL
```

He <u>studied</u> hard because he <u>had been promised</u> a car if his grades <u>were</u> good.

Place. When the adverbial clause expresses *place,* it is introduced by such connectors as "where," or "wherever." An adverbial clause expressing place indicates where the action of the verb occurs.

Examples:

```
     ┌──────────┐
     V       ADV CL
```

He always <u>stood</u> where he <u>was told.</u>

```
┌──────────────────────────────┐
ADV CL                         V
```

<u>Wherever the Vice President went,</u> he <u>was booed</u> by the crowds.

Concession. When the adverbial clause expresses *concession,* it is introduced by "although" or "even though." An adverbial clause expressing concession indicates that the action of the verb was completed despite the fact that a condition exists, existed, or will exist which is not in concert with that action.

Examples:

```
┌─────────────────────────┐
ADV CL                    V
```

Although he <u>was</u> never arrested, he <u>proclaimed</u> himself the biggest pothead in town.

```
  ┌────────┬──────────────┐
  V        V          ADV CL
```

They <u>were</u> seldom <u>seen</u> together, although they <u>claimed</u> to love each other.

Examples of sentences containing more than one adverbial clause:

Although young people have traditionally alienated themselves from adults,

they <u>must seek</u> an avenue for reconciliation today because young and old alike

                ADV CL

face common problems that must be solved if society is to continue to exist.

ADV CL   N V

Because it contained many passages of explicit passion, the book was removed

            ADV CL

from the shelves of the library after pressure from the community was brought
to bear on the administration of the school.

ADV CL   N V

If politicians do not open their eyes to the problems of modern society, it is

       V   ADV CL

conceivable that a time may come when these problems will be insoluble.

EXERCISES

1. Develop the following sentences with the structures indicated in the blanks. The best way to begin is first to read the sentence given, then to create a picture in your mind, and finally to use the undeveloped structures to express the details of your picture.

a. _____ (ADV CL—time), _____ John, _____ (APP) _____, was unable to make up his mind.

_____

_____

_____

              V-"ING"

b. The _____ (A) _____ noise, becoming louder _____ (ADV CL—time),

V

was a potential hazard to our hearing, _____ (ADV CL—concession) _____.

_____

_____

c.   (PN — time)   , the laughter   (ADJ CL)   could

be heard   (ADV CL — concession)   .

d.   (ADV CL — condition)   we will move his car   (ADV CL — reason)   .

e. The treasure found   (ADV CL — place)   would never be spent by

explorers   (ADV CL — reason)   .

2.   Choose a picture of a character from a magazine. Using the modifying structures
      learned thus far, describe his or her physical characteristics and personality as
      you see them and defend that person's right to exist.

Alternative Structures Used in Place of a Noun — Noun Clauses (N Cl)

Often clauses fit in a sentence slot normally reserved for nouns. For this reason they
are referred to as noun clauses (N Cl). Like adjective and adverbial clauses they are
sentences that have been subordinated and incorporated into the main sentence

structure. Noun clauses are usually introduced by the connectors "that," "what," "whatever" "who," "whoever," "whom," and "whomever."

Example:

N CL

Whoever designed that house is to be commended.

The sentences "He wrote the essay" (N V N) and "The use of drugs is encouraged by the devil" (N V) are subordinated by whoever and that respectively and incorporated as noun clauses in the following sentence:

N CL   V   N CL

Whoever wrote the essay has claimed that the use of drugs is encouraged by the devil.

Other examples are:

    N   V   N CL

The girl was asked whom she loved.

N CL   LV   N

That man has reached the moon is an unbelievable feat.

Noun clauses can replace a noun in a prepositional phrase. For example, in the sentence "I will give the money to the boy" the noun "boy" can be replaced by a noun clause: "I will give the money to whoever can produce a pollution-free engine."

The Infinitive ("to"-V)

An infinitive ("to"-V) is a phrase consisting of "to" followed by a verb: to sing, to dance, to live. Infinitives, like noun clauses, can substitute for a noun.

Example:

"TO"-V (N) LV   N

To sing   is an enjoyable pastime.

Infinitive phrases may be developed. To visualize how this is done you might consider the basic phrase as the sentence structure N V with the noun eliminated so that you have only V; or, when the basic phrase introduces a noun, as the sentence structure N V N with the first noun eliminated so that you have only V N.

Examples
(In the following sentences, the complete infinitive phrase has been enclosed in parentheses.)

"TO"-V

(To discover the natural beauty of the American countryside) was his fondest dream.

"TO"-V

She plans (to visit her aunt in California while on vacation).

Parallelisms

A parallelism is a series of identical structures such as two or more words, phrases, or clauses.

Words:
Animal Farm is neither a children's story nor a myth.

A knowledgeable and sensitive person is a pleasure to be around.

Honesty and sincerity and kindness are qualities I admire.

Phrases:
Leaving the city and heading for the open spaces were constantly on his mind.

He was about to lock his car and (to) enter the store when he remembered he had forgotten his wallet. The study of ghetto culture and (of) the culture of the rich convinced him of the inequities of life.

Clauses:
The de jure moral codes which some condemned as antiquated and (which) others praised as functional were binding on the citizens of the small town. That the streets are unsafe, that the number of homicides continues to grow, and that man has seemingly become insensitive to his fellow man indicate the failure of society to cope with the social dynamics of modern life.

Overview of Modifiers

Theoretically the positions of modifiers in a sentence are predictable. The following is the most common lineup of the modifiers we have studied, although it is unusual to find all of them together.

ADV CL	D A V-"ING" N PN APP V-"ING" ADJ CL	V	D A V-"ING" N PN APP V-"ING" ADJ CL PN ADV CL
	V-"ED" V-"ED"		V-"ED" V-"ED"

If you were to poll students to determine their attitude toward learning grammar, you would find that most consider the latter an exercise in futility. They have learned hundreds of rules but have been given little direction on their use. We hope that this brief survey of grammar has begun to bridge this gap between the description of grammar and its usage. Grammar should have no other purpose in the class than to ensure that you can use it as a tool to say exactly what you want. When you write your own sentences in which you incorporate the modifiers you have learned, you might be dissatisfied initially because they do not sound like "you." Don't let this discourage you, because in time this style will seem more natural than your previous one.

You have probably written a good sentence if you have followed the rules given and if the sentence is qualified so that there is no misinterpretation or undeveloped picture of what you are attempting to say.

EXERCISES

1. The following exercise is designed to show you how to analyze someone else's style by imitating it. The first step is to break down the sentence into component structures. The second step is to choose a subject on which to write. The third step is to attempt to imitate each sentence by using the same structures. It is not often possible to imitate a sentence exactly, and it might be necessary to add a structure of your own; however, in the following exercise try to imitate the style as closely as possible. Do this exercise on a separate sheet of paper.

Original Sentence:

The Presidential retreat at Camp David in Maryland's Catoctin Mountains is a special sanctuary for Richard Nixon, a personal hideway where he can find the seclusion he treasures.

Imitation:

The student cafeteria at Lux College near Long Beach is a dining haven for unsophisticated students, a noisy hole where conversations are often as insipid as the food.

Paragraph to Be Analyzed:

High above the hot plains of Tanzania's Serengeti National Park, the snowy peak of Mount Kilimanjaro glittered in the morning sun. On one gentle slope of the towering mountain, five young Africans armed with hunting rifles lay sprawled on the ground peering intently ahead. A burly white man studied them carefully for a few moments. Then he barked an order to fire. Five shots cracked through the clear air. The damage: five neat holes in as many paper targets and not a wild animal in sight. "Not bad," grinned Patrick Hemingway, 44, a white hunter who has put down the gun to teach wildlife conservation in the very shadow of the famous mountain where his father, Ernest Hemingway, once loved to hunt.*

2.   Read the following sentences and form a detailed picture in your mind of their cumulative meaning. Once you have done this, use the structures that you have studied on the preceding pages to develop each sentence with details. *Attempt to keep the original sentence intact.*

Example:
Original Sentences:
Mary lifted the telephone. Her hands trembled. However, her fears were dispelled immediately, and hot tears began to flow down her flushed face.

Developed Sentences:
After a great deal of deliberation, <u>Mary</u>, believing that time heals all wounds, <u>lifted the telephone</u>, which had sat unused for many weeks. Despite her newly found confidence, <u>her hands trembled</u> as she dialed because she realized that she was facing the possibility of her estranged husband's refusing to accept her apology. <u>However</u>, when her husband began the conversation with, "I love you," <u>her fears were dispelled immediately, and hot tears began to flow down her flushed face</u>.

    a. Lance never had a chance. He grew up as a poor farm boy. He moved to the city. He tried to better his life. Too many problems arose. The farm was his only hope. He left the city.

    b. The breach was apparent. Everyone deserted them. Mary felt the friendships could be saved. Everyone returned.

    c. Society has become enmeshed in problems. Its laws have lost favor. Only a miracle can change things. Many have tried but failed. There is only one hope left.

When we think, our minds often flash a myriad of fragmented ideas into our consciousness, and almost intuitively we understand their relationship. On the other hand, when we write, we are challenged to build transitional bridges between these fragmented ideas and thereby show their relationship because they might not be evident to the reader. The latter principle is much like the development of an outline into prose.

At the top of the following page, we have selected two sets of three sentences which were composed at random by a class and developed individually by students. These students were asked to keep the original sentence structure intact and to develop them so that they would cohere as a single impression.

---

*"The Sun Also Rises," *Newsweek*, October 16, 1972, p. 48. Copyright Newsweek, Inc., 1972; reprinted by permission.

Original sentences:
The boy was hit by a car.
It was sunny in New York.
The little old lady went home.

Developed sentences:
The boy who was riding his bike along the bridge Saturday morning was hit by a car as it changed lanes. It was sunny that day in New York, but the bright day did little to lessen the grief felt by the parents of the boy. Even the little old lady who came to the bridge because she liked to watch the ships below went home sad that afternoon.

Original sentences:
The cat died.
The boy was visibly sad.
People were seen going home.

Developed sentences:
Although he was usually careful, the cat died crossing the street one late afternoon. The boy who owned the cat, hearing the screeching of tires and running out immediately, was visibly sad as he looked down at his cat smashed against the pavement. After the cat was taken off the street, everything returned to normal and people were seen going home from work knowing little of the tragedy that had just happened.

EXERCISE

Develop the following sets of sentences as we have done above.

1.   a. The pool was full.
     b. The night was warm.
     c. We all left laughing.
2.   a. Seven years passed
     b. She arrived in town.
     c. His glasses fell off.
3.   a. The grass was wet.
     b. We were alone.
     c. The day was a blast.
4.   a. The water was hot.
     b. It didn't take us long to change our minds.
     c. Listening to records is a great pastime.

It is a mistake to associate wordy writing only with long sentences since the opposite can also be true. The passage below, from D. C. Peattie's book *Lives of Destiny*, has been paraphrased with short sentences to demonstrate how wordy short sentences can be. Your assignment, conversely, is to eliminate all expendable words by combining these sentences using some of the knowledge of modification you have learned in this section.

EXERCISE

We have combined some of the first sentences to show you the possible avenues of modification open to you. The best way to proceed on your own now is to separate groupings of sentences with hash marks (/). Revise between lines as we have done below.

In   refusing a third

/ ~~The year was~~ 1809x, Jefferson, ~~refused another~~ term of officex, ~~It would have been~~

retired

~~his third term. He retired~~ forever from politics. He went back to Monticellox, ~~Monticello~~

where   as

~~was~~ his country estatex, ~~There~~ he could exercise his diverse giftsx ~~He could be~~ an archi-

an inventor,   and

tectx, ~~He could be~~ a farmerx, ~~He could invent~~x, ~~He could be~~ a naturalistx, ~~He could be a~~

philosopher. /

Monticello is a beautiful old mansion. You may still see it in the gadgets he rigged

up. They are ingenious. You may still see the weather vane with the dial. It is in the hall.

You may still see the dumbwaiters. Also, there are the tunnels and the private stair-

cases. There is the machine which could write letters in duplicate. In addition, you may

still see the indoor-and-outdoor clock. It has cannonball counterweights. There is one

cannonball counterweight for each day of the week. At Monticello he was happy. This

in spite of tragic personal losses. His beloved wife had died in her youth. But Monti-

cello remained to him. He was ahead of his time. Her name was Martha Skelton. And four of his six children had died in their youth. But Monticello remained to him. It was

a lifelong passion. He was an ardent gardener. He was a scientific farmer. He was ahead

of his time in soil conservation. He was also very advanced in contour plowing. Indeed,

he invented a plow. It was an excellent plow. Also, he introduced corn, oats, and olives.

These were foreign plants. He introduced upland rice as well. It was another foreign

plant. He distributed these foreign plants to experimenters. These experimenters were

all over the country.

The mansion itself was thirty-five years abuilding. It was designed in detail by its

master. Jefferson was a born architect. Architecture is the most civic and logical of

the arts. Through this art he visibly expressed his power to build. This was the same

power to build which took political form too. Monticello has domes and pillars and

symmetrically balanced wings. These features fathered a certain style. That style is

called "Southern plantation."*

Introductory Transitional Words and Phrases

Some words and phrases are commonly used to provide continuity between sentences. Although overuse of some of these expressions can make writing awkward
and mechanical, when used moderately and with variety, they can improve paragraph coherence.

RELATIONSHIP	EXPRESSION
Addition, continuation	and, also, in addition, moreover, further-more, first, second, again
Contrast	but, however, nevertheless, yet, still, on

*Adapted from Donald Culross Peattie, "Thomas Jefferson, Architect of Democracy," in *Lives of Des-tiny,* Houghton Mifflin Co., Boston, and New American Library, New York, 1953, p. 21 in Signet NAL edition. Reprinted by permission of Noel R. Peattie and the Author's Agent, James Brown Associates, Inc. Copyright © 1943 by The Reader's Digest Association.

the other hand, notwithstanding, on the contrary

Exemplification, illustration	similarly, likewise, in a like manner, in the same way, in a similar case
Conclusion (result)	therefore, consequently, thus, as a result, then, hence, as a consequence
Conclusion (summation)	to sum up, in conclusion, finally, in summary, in short, in sum
Concession	although, though, even though granted that, it may be true that
Emphasis	indeed, of course, in fact, even this

EXERCISE

1. The following is a team exercise that may involve two or more students. The first student is to begin a sentence and develop it completely. He is then to begin the next sentence with a transitional phrase he has chosen from above. The second student is to complete the second sentence and begin the third with the transitional of his choice and so on. *Each student is to begin a sentence.* (Write on a separate sheet of paper.)

   Example:
   First student:
   Since the beginning of the year, I have had three accidents on the freeway. Consequently,
   Second student:
   I never drive any more if I have had a drink. However,
   First or third student:
   I have never regarded beer as a "drink." As a result,
   Second or fourth student:
   I am always getting loaded on beer and having accidents on the freeway. For example,
   First or fifth student:
   I recently piled into the back of a new station wagon. Furthermore,
   etc.

2. Write a one-page essay in which you use the transitional phrases above. Use a separate piece of paper.

   Example:
   I enjoy the mountains in the winter when the snow is deep and the slopes are

buzzing with people. <u>Furthermore</u>, I delight in the crisp air outside and the warm fireplace in the lodge. <u>In particular</u>, I like the feeling of being part of an excitement—part of a mood—that is captured only when one belongs to the ski crowd. When winter is over, <u>however</u>, I put away my skis and go searching for one of the many summer activities one can find. Swimming in the ocean, for example, etc.

chapter 10

THE PARAGRAPH: METHODS AND MODELS

To be effective, a paragraph must meet three basic requirements:

1.   It must be *unified.* That is, it must be clearly *about one thing*—namely, the one main point or idea that is generally stated at the very beginning in the *topic sentence.*

2.   It must be sufficiently *developed.* It must contain *enough* information or detail to fully "back up" the idea of the topic sentence.

3.   It must be *coherent* and make clear sense so that one sentence leads to the next in a logical way. Its words must be clear and "right," its sentences constructed for maximum intelligibility, and its transitions *between* sentences explicit wherever necessary (Turn to page 244 for a quick review of the most common transitional words and phrases.)

   Also, within an extended composition, a good paragraph will (1) develop a clear-cut *stage* of a larger topic and (2) convey an idea that is closely *related* to the idea of the paragraph that comes before it and the paragraph that comes after it.

   A topic sentence may be developed into an effective paragraph by means of:

1.   Narrative (telling a story)
2.   Description (a word picture)
3.   Example ("for instances")
4.   Comparison and contrast
5.   Cause and effect
6.   Definition
7.   Analysis
8.   Process analysis
9.   Combinations of any of these

1. NARRATIVE

Narrative—explaining an idea by telling a story—is everybody's favorite method. As soon as a child is able to talk, he says, "Tell me a story." Narrative is also the most time-honored method, far older really than the parables of Jesus or the fables of Aesop. Yet its usefulness is as fresh as the latest case history in your new psychology textbook.

Technically, a narrative is a succession of details in *time,* one thing happening after another. The time span can be compressed into minutes, or it can be stretched out over a longer period.

Obviously narrative is the main vehicle of stories and novels, and in those forms the use of the topic sentence is often unnecessary; the topic idea usually is something the author wishes his readers to discover for themselves as an experience. But narrative is just as appropriate to all types of writing which require the clear demonstration of an explicitly stated idea.

In the following examples, the topic sentences have been italicized.

a.

On the very evening, when the King came up, Bruce did a brave act that encouraged his men. He was seen by a certain Henry de Bohun, an English Knight, riding about before his army on a little horse, with a light battle-ax in his hand, and a crown of gold on his head. This English Knight, who was mounted on a strong warhorse, cased in steel, strongly armed, and able (as he thought) to overthrow Bruce by crushing him with his mere weight, set spurs to his great charger, rode on him and made a thrust at him with his heavy spear. Bruce parried the thrust, and with one blow of his battle-ax split his skull.

—Charles Dickens, *A Child's History of England*

b.

For a long time it was quiet. Benjamin sat looking down at the rug. Once he glanced up at his mother, who was sitting in her chair watching him, then he looked for a moment at his father's shoes and quickly back at the rug in front of him. His mother cleared her throat. Mr. Robinson moved slightly on the couch beside him. Then it was perfectly quiet again.

—Charles Webb, *The Graduate**

* Charles Webb, *The Graduate,* The New American Library, New York. This excerpt is from p. 59 of the Signet Books edition.

2. DESCRIPTION

While narrative follows a time sequence, description takes us through *space*. Within a descriptive paragraph we simply guide our reader from one point in space to the next in the most natural order possible. And since the greatest part of our awareness is of things seen, most descriptive writing is concerned with visual space. We try to make our reader see what we see as surely as if we were sending him a snapshot of the subject.

c.

It was the hour of twilight on a soft spring day toward the end of April in the year of Our Lord 1929, and George Webber leaned his elbows on the sill of his back window and looked out at what he could see of New York. His eye took in the towering mass of the new hospital at the end of the block, its upper floors set back in terraces, the soaring walls salmon colored in the evening light. This side of the hospital, and directly opposite, was the lower structure of the annex, where the nurses and the waitresses lived. In the rest of the block half a dozen old brick houses, squeezed together in a solid row, leaned wearily against each other and showed their backsides to him.

—Thomas Wolfe, *You Can't Go Home Again**

d.

We drove out to the surf house in separate cars. It was on the sea at the good end of town: a pueblo hotel whose Spanish gardens were dotted with hundred-dollar-a-day cottages. The terraces in front of the main building descended in wide green steps to its own marina. Yachts and launches were bobbing at the slips. Further out on the water, beyond the curving promontory that gave Pacific Point its name, white sails leaned against a low gray wall of fog.

—Ross Macdonald, *The Chill*†

e.

1644 West 54th Place was a dried-out brown house with a dried-out brown

---

* From p. 3 in *You Can't Go Home Again* by Thomas Wolfe, Harper & Row, New York, 1940.

† Ross MacDonald, *The Chill*, Alfred A. Knopf, Inc., New York, 1963. Copyright © 1963 by Ross Mac-Donald. Excerpt is from p. 8 of Bantam Books edition.

lawn in front of it. There was a large bare patch around a tough-looking palm tree. On the porch stood one lonely wooden rocker, and the afternoon breeze made the unpruned shoots of last year's poinsettias tap-tap against the cracked stucco wall. A line of stiff yellowish half-washed clothes jittered on a rusty wire in the side yard.

—Raymond Chandler, *Farewell, My Lovely**

Observe in the three preceding examples the skillful arrangement of details. Each paragraph begins with a topic statement that gives a general impression of the place being described, just as a film sequence usually starts with an "establishing" long shot. Then our attention is directed to those secondary details that would follow most naturally (and logically) were we sharing the point of view of the narrator. Specifically, in paragraph c this is a movement from background (the large hospital at the end of the block) to foreground (the annex) to an in-between area; in d, on the other hand, it is a movement from foreground (hotel and terraces) to background (the marina, then the slips, then the promontory, and finally the white sails); and in e it is a movement from the bare lawn and its tree to the porch behind it to the wall adjoining the porch to the yard at the side—that is, a shift from one side to another. Also, in each case there is a general movement from objects of more significance to those of less.

Observe, too, the care each of these writers has taken to make his details touch our senses. We are not given mere dry information about a big hospital; instead, we are made to experience its "soaring walls salmon colored in the evening light." These authors make us see:

Yachts and launches were bobbing at the slips. . . .

. . . white sails leaned against a low wall of fog.

. . . the afternoon breeze made the unpruned shoots of last year's poinsettias tap-tap against the cracked stucco wall

A line of stiff yellowish half-washed clothes jittered on a rusty wire in the side yard.

Descriptions of people are more complicated than descriptions of things or places. A man or woman is rarely reducible to mere physical size, contours, and coloring as is a table or chair. Usually we want to know something about his or her background, personality, and social situation. Indeed, the nineteenth-century novelist Balzac made exhaustive use of descriptions of settings precisely as a means of clarifying his characters' personalities. Here is his picture of Madame Vauquer, the proprietress of a down-at-heels lodging house in Paris:

f.

Her dining room is at the height of its splendor when, toward seven o'clock in the morning, Madame Vauquer's cat precedes its mistress, leaps on the sideboards, sniffs at the milk in several bowls covered with plates, and enjoys its morning purr. Soon the widow follows, arrayed in a tulle cap under which is a mass of false hair ill-arranged; as she walks she drags her slippers which have lost their shape. Here is an oldish, fattish face with a parrot's nose in the center; her plump little hands, her body fat as a church rat's, her prominent pendulous breasts, all are in harmony with this room which is dripping with unhappiness, vacant of all speculation, and full of warm stale air which Madame Vauquer breathes without any sense of disgust.

In the paragraph immediately following this one, Balzac is even more explicit about the relationship between the character and her setting.

g.

That face of hers, as nipping as the first autumn frost, those wrinkled eyes, whose expression shifts from the smile required of dancers to the bitter frown of the cashier, indeed her whole person gives the clue to the boarding-house, just as the boarding-house implies such a mistress as Madame Vauquer. You cannot imagine a jail without a jailer. The unhealthy obesity of this little woman is the product of this life of hers, just as typhus fever is the product of the exhalations in a hospital. Her skirt is made of an old dress, and through its rents the wadding projects; beneath it falls her woolen petticoat; and these clothes sum up the drawing room, the dining room, the little garden, explain the kitchen and give an idea of the borders. The moment she is here, the spectacle is complete.

—Honoré de Balzac, *Père Goriot**

A more modern character description, from the hard-boiled school of detective fiction, is given at the top of page 252.

*Honoré de Balzac, *Père Goriot*, translated by E. K. Brown, Dorothea Walter, and John Watkins, Random House, New York, 1946, pp. 8–9. Copyright 1946, 1950 by Random House, Inc.

h.

She was about twenty-eight years old. She had a rather narrow forehead
of more height than is considered elegant. Her nose was small and in-
quisitive, her upper lip a shade too long and her mouth more than a
shade too wide. Her eyes were gray-blue with flecks of gold in them.
She had a nice smile. She looked as if she had slept well. It was a nice
face, a face you get to like. Pretty, but not so pretty that you would have
to wear brass knuckles every time you took it out.

—Raymond Chandler, *Farewell, My Lovely**

3. EXAMPLE

The simplest way to develop a topic sentence is by the use of examples—a series
of "for instances."

i.

Leonardo's inventions are endless. He designed an earth drill, prefabricated
portable houses, rolling mills, a screw-cutting machine, a boring machine, a bulldozer, a cement mixer, a spinning machine, and a harbor
dredge. He was the first man to construct a graph to represent a mathe-
matical fact, the first to propose armored ships or suggest the use of steam
power, to mount a magnetic needle on a horizontal axis, thereby giving
us the compass as we know it today. And he was the inventor of what we
now call a differential gear. He tinkered with cogs to count the re-
volutions of a wheel, like the mileage clock on our motor cars, and invented an anemometer or wind-gauge.

—Donald Culross Peattie, *Lives of Destiny*†

Obviously no predetermined order—such as the time order in a narrative or the
space order in a description—is required for this kind of development. Still, an ef-

*Raymond Chandler, *Farewell, My Lovely,* Alfred A. Knopf, Inc., New York, 1940. Copyright 1940 by
Raymond Chandler, renewed 1968 by Helga Greene, executrix of the estate of Raymond Chandler.
Excerpt is from p. 64 of Pocket Books edition (Simon & Schuster).

†Adapted from Donald Culross Peattie, "Leonardo da Vinci," in *Lives of Destiny,* Houghton Mifflin Co.,
Boston, and New American Library, New York, 1953, p. 104 in Signet NAL edition. Reprinted by permission of Noel R. Peattie and the Author's Agent, James Brown Associates, Inc., Copyright © 1943
by The Reader's Digest Association.

fective presentation of illustrative examples is not a random one. Consider the various patterns in which the details in paragraph i have been arranged.

4. COMPARISON AND CONTRAST

As we stated earlier, nothing viewed in isolation is half so interesting as when it is viewed alongside something else.

j.

The three models differ somewhat in the available accessories. The flashgun furnished with the top-priced *250* costs an extra $8.50 with the other two. For all three, you can buy a cable release ($2.20), self-timer ($5.95), development timer ($7.50) and several types of cases ($8.50 to $19.95). For the *230* and *250,* but not the *210,* there are close-up attachments ($9.95 and $10.95, respectively), a filter to accentuate clouds in black-and-white pictures ($5.95) and a filter to lighten outdoor shadows in color pictures ($4.50)

—*Consumer Reports**

k.

But women have always had a greater capacity to feign satisfaction than have men. In times of change, men's refusal to put up with any more of whatever they feel they have had enough of is infinitely valuable. Thus, we may see the long hair of boys today, the fine feathers, and the refusal to take part in a system that is seen as archaic. At the moment it gives females short shrift, but at least they have been educated, they can participate in what is going on; a girl need no longer, as one small girl phrased it, "sit up in the tower waiting for her knight to come riding by." She can be right down there beside him fighting the dragons.

—Margaret Mead, "Where American Women Are Now"†

Note that paragraph j presents an item-by-item contrast and paragraph k an over-

---

* "Polaroid Camera," *Consumer Reports,* vol. XXX (January, 1968), p. 46. Copyright 1968 by Consumers Union of United States, Inc., Mount Vernon, New York 10550. Reprinted by permission from CONSUMER REPORTS, January 1968.

† Margaret Mead, "Where American Women Are Now," *Vogue,* May 1969.

all contrast (first men, then women). Usually the nature of the subject will determine the method adopted.

Although the above comparisons are developed with examples, other methods may also be used. Two houses may be contrasted by means of pure description; two styles of bowling or golfing may be compared by means of parallel narratives, and so on.

5. CAUSE AND EFFECT

Especially useful in scholarly and scientific writing is the movement from cause to effect or from effect to cause. In biology we are often told of the bizarre behavior of some animal then made to understand the reasons for his behavior. And arguments in philosophy and the social sciences are frequently systematic demonstrations of causes yielding certain inevitable results.

1.

If we adopt a broader perspective of foreign trade we find that a country's standard of living is nearly always improved by free trade relations, and harmed by tariffs and other artificial trade restrictions. The fundamental basis of foreign trade is international cost differences. Under free trade a country will import goods produced more cheaply abroad than at home, and export those produced more cheaply at home than abroad. This necessarily means that the people of a country will have more goods and services for their productive efforts than they would if trade were restricted. Since the volume of goods and services available to a society on a per capita basis is the economic measure of its standard of living, it follows that free trade is one of the important ways for a country to raise its standard of living.

—Delbert A. Snyder, *Economic Myth and Reality**

6. DEFINITION

The careful definition is at least as crucial to intellectual argumentation as the cause and effect demonstration. However, the technique of building upon a definition is equally at home in all types of writing, no matter how breezy or frivolous their intent.

---

* Delbert A. Snider, *Economic Myth and Reality,* © 1965, p. 95, Prentice-Hall, Inc., Englewood Cliffs, New Jersey.

m.

*It is quite true that the artist, painter, writer or composer starts always with
an experience that is a kind of discovery. He comes upon it with the sense of a
discovery; in fact, it is true to say that it comes upon him as a discovery. This is
what is usually called an intuition or an inspiration.* It carries with it always
the feeling of directness. For instance, you go walking in the fields and all
at once they strike you in quite a new aspect; you find it extraordinary
that they should be like that. This is what happened to Monet as a young
man. He suddenly saw the fields, not as solid flat objects covered with
grass or useful crops and dotted with trees, but as colour in astonishing
variety and subtlety of gradation. And this gave him a delightful and
quite new pleasure. It was a most exciting discovery, especially as it was a
discovery of something real. I mean, by that, something independent
of Monet himself. That, of course, was half the pleasure. Monet had
discovered a truth about the actual world.

—Joyce Cary, *Art and Reality: Ways of the Creative Process**

7. ANALYSIS

Analysis is the subdivision of something into its component parts, whether that
something is a group of people, the goods in a warehouse, or the ideas set forth in a
political speech. It is a kind of description in the abstract, its details moving in
"mental" space.

n.

Aid has two polical functions. The first is to act as a "holding operation"
in areas where, because of an economic crisis, political and social stability
are threatened and the society is open to communist infiltration. The
second is to act as a long-run design to help create economic foundations
for the maintenance and development of democratic ideas and institutions.

—Delbert A. Snyder, *Economic Myth and Reality*†

---

*From pp. 1–2 in *Art and Reality* by Joyce Cary, Volume Twenty of World Perspectives Series, planned
and edited by Ruth Nanda Anshen, Harper & Row, New York, 1958.

†Delbert A. Snider, *Economic Myth and Reality,* © 1965, p. 108, Prentice-Hall, Inc., Englewood Cliffs,
New Jersey.

8. PROCESS ANALYSIS

To analyze a process or a flow of events is to explain it as a series of "steps." In a sense, this technique is a kind of controlled narrative. Process analysis carries the burden of much historical writing (how it happened), and it is also the primary method of most technical writing (how to do it), familiarly exemplified by the do-it-yourself manual and the cookbook.

o.

TEA, PROPERLY POURED

To serve each guest, set teacup on dessert plate. Pour tea, adding lemon, milk or cream, and sugar as guest prefers. Place spoon on plate at back of cup, with its handle parallel to handle of cup; pass to guest, with napkin beneath plate. Let guests help themselves to the tea snack; or have a guest pass it; or pass it yourself after all have been served tea.

— *The New Good Housekeeping Cookbook**

In addition, the humorous or satiric possibilities of this device are remarkable. Witness the best-selling manual, *How to Be a Jewish Mother.*

9. COMBINATIONS OF ANY OF THESE

We have already suggested that a comparison-contrast paragraph can be built upon description or narrative as well as straight examples. Why not also compare or contrast extended definitions, cause-effect units, and so forth? And normally a cause-effect unit is, in itself, a blend of examples incorporating narrative and descriptive and analytical elements. Indeed, the possibilities of all these techniques are practically unlimited.

EXERCISES

1.   *Narrative:* Using sample paragraph a as a model, write a narrative paragraph about some notable instance of human heroism or endeavor. This may be based upon an incident that you have witnessed, one that you have heard or read about, or one

---

*Dorothy B. Marsh, Ed., *The New Good Housekeeping Cookbook,* 1963 edition, p. 75, Copyright © 1963 by The Hearst Corporation. Reprinted by permission.

that you have simply imagined. Whatever your approach, be sure to include enough detail to make your story interesting and believable. Also, be careful to keep your flow of events uninterrupted. Begin with a topic sentence.

Using b as a model, illustrate some very normal, everyday situation with a narrative paragraph. Begin with a topic sentence.

2. *Description:* Using paragraphs c, d, and e as models, write a description of some nearby exterior scene. You might simply look out your classroom window or, if necessary, step outside to the nearest stairway or veranda. Your subject should be somewhat challenging—a bit more complex than a water hose or lamppost. Begin by analyzing the scene, even to the point of sketching a little map or picture, so that your details will emerge in the most natural and logical order. Again, a movement from primary to secondary to incidental details is usually best. Remember to make your details as clear and vivid as possible. Imagine a reader in France or Thailand struggling to *see* something. Give him a true word picture. Begin your paragraph with a topic sentence, a "long shot" of your entire subject.

Using f and h as models, describe some student in your group or class. (Two rows of chairs may be arranged to face each other.) Withhold the name of your subject from your paragraph; let others try to determine whom you have written about. Begin with a topic sentence.

Write a few brief descriptive details that touch as many senses as possible (touch, smell, sound, taste, but especially sight). Consult the examples on pages 249–252 for suggestions; also consider such possibilities as food, mountain vistas, or grotesquely ugly things. Whatever you do, try to arouse strong feelings in your reader. To achieve this, you must concentrate on language; there is simply no substitute for the perfect word or phrase.

3. *Examples:* Using i as a model, develop some general statement with a series of clearly relevant examples. Select a subject area with which you are quite familiar. Your details should come readily to hand.

4. *Comparison and contrast:* Using k as a model, compare a first impression of someone you have known with a later impression of that person. That is, in the first half of the paragraph, thoroughly describe this person as he first struck you (his appearance and behavior and your feelings about him); then, in the second half, tell how he struck you a week (a month, a year) later. Was your first impression justified? Not justified? All wrong? Begin with a topic sentence. (Example: Geniuses sometimes have feet of clay.)

Alternative assignments: Compare two different people, or describe one person as a stranger might expect him to be compared with what he really is.

5. *Cause and Effect:* Using paragraph i as a model, briefly relate some weird or unexpected fact of nature or human nature (this will be your topic sentence), and then explain the reasons for it (this will be the bulk of your support).

As a variation on the above, begin with a cause and then explain its effects.

6. *Definition:* Using m as a model, explain some very ordinary thing by defining it. Such a paragraph might begin, "A motorcycle is the perfect sweetheart" or "Love is not so much an emotion as a mechanical reflex." Each of these statements cries out for further elaboration.

7. *Analysis:* Using n as a model, analyze the members of your class or school into five distinct types (or seven or nine—you decide). Begin with a topic sentence stating the terms of the analysis.

8. *Process analysis:* Using o as a model, write an *original* how-to-do-it paragraph on any subject. Make your "steps" clear and precise. A typical topic sentence: "Shaving can be accomplished in six easy steps."

9. *Combinations of any of these:* Experiment!

DISCUSSION: Read all paragraph exercises aloud in your group (or class). Does each adhere to the prescribed format? If some are remarkably more effective than others, ask why.

chapter 11

RULES FOR PUNCTUATION

THE COMMA

Rule 1

Use a comma after introductory phrases and clauses.

Examples:
At the entrance to the stadium, scalpers could be seen making their last-minute pitches.

Turning to a life of crime to support his habit, the addict alienated himself still further from society.

When he surveyed the conditions of the poor, he found another America.

Exception: A short, single, introductory prepositional phrase need not be followed by a comma unless it is parenthetical (*in addition*, or *on the other hand*) or helps keep the sentence's meaning clear.

Examples:
In time we will find our destinies. (Short prepositional phrase.)

On the other hand, you could say that women have too many rights. (Parenthetical expression.)

In winter, sports are often played inside. (Without a comma after it, winter seems to modify sports.)

Rule 2

Use a comma after introductory words like, "no," "yes," "well," or "why."

Examples:
No, he can't be right.
Well, I find it hard to believe.

Rule 3

Use commas to separate three or more similar words, phrases, or clauses in a series. When there is a conjunction between the last two words or phrases it is optional to place a comma between them, unless the omission will make the sentence unclear.

> Examples:
> Broken windows, scattered cigarette butts (,) and dirty glasses were the aftermath of the raucous party.
>
> His dream was to build a race car, race at "Indy(,)" and retire a millionaire.
>
> A club that collected newspapers, sold bottles, and did odd jobs to raise money for the poor was commended in today's paper.

Rule 4

Use a comma to separate independent clauses joined by a coordinating conjunction (and, but, or, nor, for), unless the clauses are short and closely related.

> Examples:
> The Los Angeles Rams made a touchdown and the "Super Bowl" became history. (The clauses in this sentence are short and closely related.)
>
> I saw my first large city at the age of twelve when I first visited Los Angeles, and I still remember the awe that its vastness awoke in me. (The clauses are long; for this reason, a comma is needed.)
>
> Exception: *Always* use a comma to separate independent clauses (double sentences) joined by "for," to avoid confusion.
>
> Example:
> The mechanic was sent, for the car had stalled again. (If the comma is omitted, it reads that the mechanic was sent for the car.)

EXERCISES

Enter commas where needed in the following sentences.

1. Until peace is found there can only be bitterness among the young confusion among adults and blood in the streets.

2. Well despite the fact that Japan was a devestated country it has become an industrial giant for its people are dedicated to this purpose.

3. Lying about his accomplishments his ambitions and his wealth the middle-aged

man was able to obtain a loan from the woman but he ultimately failed to win her heart.

4.   Despite the many terrifying dreams he had he was able to keep his sanity.

5.   At night he listened to the wind twisting its way through the branches of the pine trees outside.

Rule 5

Use commas to set off a nonessential adjective clause or phrase. A nonessential adjective clause or phrase is one that adds information about a noun but can be omitted without changing the basic meaning of the sentence. Essential adjective clauses and phrases are never set apart by commas, for without their presence the sentence would be confusing.

Examples:
Nonessential:
The Grand Canyon, which has been acclaimed one of the most scenic natural wonders of the world, is in Arizona.

The news media, which have become a powerful voice in this country, have been attacked repeatedly by irresponsible politicians.

The president of the college, knowing of the plan by dissidents to disrupt classes, sought to meet privately with them.

NOTE: There is a distinct pause before and after each nonessential element. This is another way of recognizing them within a sentence.

Essential·
Most students that attend UCLA come from California.

Speeches given by the President are of interest to Americans and aliens as well.

The man chasing the cat fell down.

Rule 6

Use commas to set off an interrupter or parenthethic expression within a sentence.

Conjunctive adverbs (moreover, consequently, therefore) used parenthetically are set off by commas.

Examples:
His objection, consequently, was the final blow to the proposal.

Moreover, I will not speak to them again.

Parenthetical transitional words and phrases are usually set off by commas.

Examples:
The university, for example, has become a scapegoat for politicians.

His salary, of course, is inadequate.

Appositives that are parenthetical should be set off by commas.

Examples:
Sam Yorty, the maverick mayor of Los Angeles, is a world traveler.

The Golden Gate Bridge, a towering monument of human ingenuity, attracts thousands of tourists each year.

Words in direct address are parenthetical and should be set off by commas.

Examples:
The provisions for the trip, John, are your concern.

Success, young man, can be measured only by the amount of self-fulfillment one has achieved.

Rule 7

Use a comma to separate items in dates. Separate the name of a day from the date and the month, and the date of the month from the year. A comma should go after the year if a period is not called for.

Examples:
The meeting on Friday, November 5, 1970, was in the files of the FBI.

The Broadway production began on September 9, 1959.

Rule 8

Use commas to separate items in addresses. Separate the name of a person or an establishment from the street address, the street address from the city, and the city from the state. Do not use a comma to separate the state from the zip code.

Example:
Send the package to Rio Hondo College, 3600 Workman Mill Road, Whittier, California 90608.

Students at U.S.C. in Los Angeles, California, must go through a ghetto to get to school.

EXERCISES

Enter commas where needed in the following sentences.

1. Malnutrition despair and fear all products of poverty afflict too many Americans.
2. Moreover there is a sense of worthlessness which dampens the spirit.
3. *Love Story* a novel about two young college students has been the object of lavish ridicule and praise.
4. On June 17 1971 Jim Stone a rookie from Notre Dame was signed by the Oakland Raiders.
5. The police tipped off by a telephone call raided the residence at 703 La Flora Drive Alhambra California but found no one there.
6. After the failure of his first attempt Charlie a small mongrel dog on our block refused to jump the fence.
7. The car which slid off the road was recovered weeks later.
8. Considering everything the student production of *The Zoo Story* a play by Edward Albee was a worthwhile undertaking.
9. Why the book was not even mine.
10. After a great deal of deliberation the committee accepted the award.

THE SEMICOLON

Rule 1

Use a semicolon between two independent clauses (double sentences) joined by such words as "accordingly," "also," "besides," "consequently," "furthermore," "hence," "however," "indeed," "instead," "moreover," "nevertheless," "otherwise," "similarly," "still," "therefore," "thus," "for example," "for instance," "that is," and "in fact."

Examples:
The weather was inclement; <u>however</u>, the game was not postponed.

The plans for my future are always changing; <u>in fact</u>, they were modified dramatically this very day.

Rule 2

Use a semicolon between independent clauses when the conjunction has been omitted.

Examples:
His arrival was a social blunder; the host found it hard to hide his anger.

I was willing to forgive; you were not.

Rule 3

A semicolon is often used to separate independent clauses if there are commas within the clauses.

Example:
The declaration of peace, the only logical step to take in view of the horror the war perpetrated, was drawn up; and there was rejoicing in the streets of the occupied country.

Rule 4

Use a semicolon between items in a series if the items contain commas.

Example:
January 7, 1972; June 3, 1972; and December 9, 1972, were the dates of our board meetings for the year 1972.

THE COLON

Rule 1

Use a colon before a list of items unless the list immediately follows a verb or preposition, in which case no punctuation is usually necessary.

Example:
The questionnaire asked the following questions: How many showers do you take per week? How much do you earn? Is your housing adequate?

Rule 2

Use a colon between independent clauses when the second explains or restates the idea of the first.

Example:
The roles he played were varied: he portrayed a pope, a killer, a tramp, and a tycoon.

THE DASH

The dash has similar uses to those of commas. It should not be confused with the hyphen, which is only a spelling device.

Rule 1

Use dashes to set off a parenthetic expression that (1) is especially emphatic or (2) contains commas of its own or (3) constitutes a sentence by itself.

Examples:
More students—58 percent more than in 1961—are going to graduate school after receiving their B.A.

Only one man—and he was chosen by the academic senate—will represent the school at the meeting.

Rule 2

Use a dash to set off an expression at the end of a sentence that might be considered a delayed afterthought.

Example:
After the snake dance the skies became cloudy and rain began to fall—an occurrence too coincidental to attribute to chance.

Rule 3

Use a dash to mean and take the place of such expressions as "namely," "in other words," and "that is" that precede explanations.

Example:
The decision of the workers not to strike was based on previous experience— the last strike lasted three years.

NOTE: In the sentence above, the dash and colon can be interchanged.

PARENTHESES

Rule 1

Use parentheses to separate parenthetical expressions that add information and are not a part of the basic construction of the sentence.

Example:
The rebel priest (a product of modern society and its changing needs) has greatly questioned the power of the Pope.

Rule 2

Use parentheses to enclose numerals or letters used to number items in a series.

Example:
Today's middle-class family has (1) more money to spend on recreation, (2) more leisure time in which to spend this money, and (3) more choices for recreation than it did twenty years ago.

NOTE: Punctuation marks are used within parentheses when they belong with the parenthetical expression. Punctuation marks that belong with the main part of the sentence are placed outside of the closing parenthesis.

Example:
During his four years of college (1965–1969), he majored in "fun."

ITALICS (UNDERLINING)

Rule 1

Use italics for titles of books, films, works of art, periodicals, and newspapers and for names of ships, spaceships, and trains.

The Godfather
Mona Lisa
Newsweek
the *Intrepid*

Rule 2

Use italics for words and letters referred to as such and for foreign words.

Examples:
The *o* in *hot* is short.

A *fait accompli* is an act which has already been accomplished or decided upon.

Rule 3

Use italics sparingly for emphasis.

Example:
The question is *when.*

QUOTATION MARKS

Rule 1

Quotation marks are used to enclose titles of chapters, articles, other parts of books or magazines, short poems, short stories, and songs.

> Examples:
> "The Killers" (Short story)
> "The Too-Late Born" (Poem)
> "The Secrets of Sesame Street" (Article in *Look*)

Rule 2

Quotation marks are used to set off words used in a special sense or from a special vocabulary. It is now optional to enclose slang with quotation marks.

> Examples:
> Tom was looked upon as a "savior" by his friends. (*Savior* is used in a special sense.)
>
> The "bull" market was to his liking. (*Bull* is part of the specialized vocabulary of Wall Street.)

Rule 3

Quotation marks are used to enclose a direct quotation.

> Example:
> Mom said, "Don't go home."

If the direct quotation is a sentence, it begins with a capital letter. If it is only a sentence fragment, no capital letter is required.

> Examples:
> When forced to retreat, the captain vowed, "We shall return." (Complete sentence.)
>
> What did he mean by "black power"? (Sentence fragment.)

Unless it supplies essential detail or is only a phrase, a direct quotation is set off from the rest of the sentence by commas or by a question mark or exclamation point.

Examples:

The phrase "It's all over between us" kept echoing in his tormented mind. (The direct quotation, a complete sentence, supplies essential detail.)

"Be careful!" he heard his mother call out. (The direct quotation is a complete sentence.)

After speaking to his parents, he comprehended what the "generation gap" meant. (The quotation is a sentence fragment.)

Commas and periods are *always* placed inside the closing quotation marks.

Example:

"Because of the poverty I saw today," he said, "I cannot eat the steak in good conscience."

Semicolons and colons are *always* placed outside the closing quotation marks.

Examples:

John was quoted as saying, "Mary is no girl friend of mine"; however, he soon changed his mind.

You can say something about "rolling stones": They are in danger of self-destruction.

Question marks and exclamation points are placed inside the closing quotation marks if they belong with the quotation; otherwise they are placed outside.

Examples:

"Who will go next?" the general asked.
Didn't you promise, "I'll return soon"?
Don't you ever tell me, "She is a coward"!

Use single quotation marks to enclose a quotation within a quotation.

Example:

"What do you make of the message 'Skies are dull'?" asked the general.

THE APOSTROPHE

Rule 1

To form the possessive case of a singular noun, add an apostrophe and an *s*. To form the possessive case of a singular noun ending in an *s* or an *s* sound and a plural noun ending in *s,* add only the apostrophe.

Examples:
The boy's hat. (Singular noun.) The boys' hat. (Plural noun.)
The witness' testimony. (Singular noun ending in *s.*)
The men's store. (Plural noun ending in a letter other than *s.*)

Rule 2

Personal pronouns in the possessive case (his, hers, its, ours, your, theirs, and whose) do not require an apostrophe. Indefinite pronouns (one, everyone, and everybody) in the possessive case require an apostrophe and *s.*

Rule 3

Each of the names of two or more persons possessing something individually takes the possessive form.

Example:
Johnson's and Nixon's administrations were characterized by protests against the war.

Note: Use the possessive on only the last name when the persons possess collectively.

Example:
John and Mary's marriage is a failure.

chapter 12

MINIEXERCISES

SPELLING LESSON

Contractions

Contractions are two words (a pronoun and some form of a verb, such as to be) which are fused into one word. In such a fusion, a letter or letters are dropped and replaced by an apostrophe. The following are examples of such words:

PRONOUN		VERB ("TO"-V)		CONTRACTION
we	+	are	=	we're (The *a* is replaced by an apostrophe.)
I	+	am	=	I'm (The *a* is replaced by an apostrophe.)
he	+	is	=	he's (The *i* is replaced by an apostrophe.)
we	+	have	=	we've (The *ha* is replaced by an apostrophe.)

EXERCISES

Combine the words enclosed by parentheses in the following sentences in the blanks provided.

1. (I have) _____ gotten over my cold.
2. (he is) _____ not here.
3. (She will) _____ come.
4. (We have) _____ decided not to.
5. (It is) _____ possible.
6. (We will) _____ answer soon.
7. (Who is) _____ coming?
8. (They are) _____ ready.
9. (Who will) _____ determine the amount?
10. (You are) _____ right.

Words That Sound Alike

Often, the only way to remember the spelling differences between words that sound alike is to invent memory tricks (mnemonic devices). For example, to remember that the word "there" means place, remember the phrase "*here* and *there*." In groups of three people, learn the meanings of the following words and devise memory tricks to remember their spellings.

1. *Whether* (if)
    He was asked whether he cared.
    Weather (atmospheric conditions)
    The weather outside is fine for football.

2. *Deer* (an animal)
    He shot the deer.
    Dear (a salutation, description, or term of affection)
    Dear Miss Jones:
    Miss Jones was a dear girl.
    I love you, dear.

3. *Here* (place)
    The car should be parked here.
    Hear (to listen)
    Did you hear the noise?

4. *Its* (possession)
    Its motor isn't very good.
    It's (it is)
    It's going to rain tonight.

5. *Then* (at that time)
    He then began to sing.
    Than (in reference to)
    Jim is stronger than Tom.

6. *Two* (number)
    There are two reasons why.
    To (*toward* or part of an infinitive)
    He went to the store.
    To hate is the opposite of to love.
    Too (in excess, also)
    He is too big.
    He, too, is a candidate.

7. *Your* (possession)
    This is your room.
    You're (you are)
    You're late!

8.   *Whose* (possession)
      Whose car is this?
      Who's (who is)
      Who's coming?

9.   *There* (place)
      The mailbox is there.
      Their (possession)
      Their dinner has arrived.

10.   *Already* (previously)
      He has already decided to go.
      All ready (all prepared or in readiness)
      He is all ready for the exam.

IMPROMPTU DRAMA

Choose people to act out the following situations.

1. An irate girl catches her boyfriend with another girl at an expensive restaurant. She is particularly angry because he has never taken her to any eating place fancier than McDonald's.

2. A girl is trying to convince a service station attendant to fix a flat tire on her car, which is some distance away. He refuses. The girl's girl friend, who is also present, becomes irate.

3. A mother and father are trying to talk their daughter out of dating a certain boy.

4. A young man or woman is trying to convince a bank officer to lend him or her $2,000.

HUMOROUS WRITING

1. Write a humorous will in which you leave your possessions to individual members of your class.

2. Invent three humorous titles for books that you would find in the libraries of the following people:
    a. The mayor of New York.
    b. The President of the United States.
    c. Your English teacher.
    d. Raquel Welch.
    e. Ralph Nader.

3. Write a humorous eulogy for someone in your class. Then write three possible epitaphs for his (her) gravestone.

WRITING EXERCISES

1. Imagine yourself an object, such as a grain of sand on a beach, a mirror, a shoe, a telephone, or a car. Write a brief essay from such a perspective.
2. Assume you are a security blanket. Describe the person you would like to be a security blanket for and the benefits of such a relationship.
3. Form groups of four students. Now divide each group into groups of two. Each person in each group will now write a story which includes the two people in the other group as characters. When the stories are done, they should be read to the entire group of four.

METAPHORS

Making Metaphors

A good writer is often considered one who can present his ideas clearly, precisely, and logically. A great writer, on the other hand, is defined as one who, going one step further, has the ability to sprinkle his writing with metaphorical associations. These associations are relationships established between things which in isolation are not evidently related. For example, in the sentence, "The ship plowed its way through the treacherous sea," the ship is compared to a plow and given, as a result, the attributes usually associated with it.

In the following example from his story "The Ice Palace," F. Scott Fitzgerald conveys a beautiful image with metaphorical associations.

> The sunlight dripped over the house like golden paint over an art jar, and the freckling shadows here and there only intensified the rigor of the bath of light. The Butterworth and Larkin houses flanking were intrenched behind great stodgy trees; only the Happer house took the full sun, and all day long faced the dusty road-street with a tolerant kindly patience. This was the city of Tarleton in southernmost Georgia, September afternoon.*

The associations are made between sunlight and paint, shadows and freckles, and the house and a person with patience.

*Excerpt from "The Ice Palace" by F. Scott Fitzgerald from BABYLON REVISITED AND OTHER STORIES is reprinted with the permission of Charles Scribner's Sons. Copyright, 1920, by Curtis Publishing Company.

The following are additional examples taken from the writings of Lawrence Durrell and Stephen Crane:

> And when night falls and the white city lights up the thousand candelabra of its parks and buildings, turns in the soft unearthly drum-music of Morrocco or Caucasus, it looks like some great crystal liner asleep there, anchored to the horn of Africa—her diamond and fire-opal reflections twisting downward like polished bars into the oily harbour among the battleships.*

> As the men trooped heavily back into the front room, the two little windows presented views of a turmoiling sea of snow. The huge arms of the wind were making attempts—mighty, circular, futile—to embrace the flakes as they sped. A gate-post like a still man with a blanched face stood aghast amid this profligate fury.†

EXERCISE

Choose a partner. Now describe him, using a metaphorical association.

Metaphors As Definitions

Metaphors can be useful as definitions. Using this concept, complete the following definitions as shown by the examples.

1. Love is over when . . .

    Example:
    Love is over when you go to a drive-in to *see* a movie.

    a. _____

    _____

    b. _____

---

*From the book BALTHAZAR by Lawrence Durrell. Copyright © 1958 by Lawrence Durrell. Published by E. P. Dutton & Co., Inc., and used with their permission and the permission of Faber and Faber, Ltd., Publishers, London.

†Stephen Crane, "The Blue Hotel," quoted from Hans P. Gath, Ed., *Literature*, 2d ed., Wadsworth Publishing Company, Belmont, California, 1968, p. 208.

_____

c. _____

_____

2.   Happiness is . . .

Example:
Happiness is finding that the "grass" you were busted for was from somebody's lawn.

a _____

_____

b. _____

_____

c. _____

_____

3.   A loser is . . .

Example:
A loser is a groom who gets a hernia carrying his bride across the threshold.

a. _____

_____

b. _____

_____

c. _____

_____

Pictures As Metaphors

In the space provided, outline three properties that a utopia possesses. Then symbo-
lise these characteristics pictorially to create a design for the flag in Figure 12-1.
Draw your design on the flag.

Figure 12-1 The flag of Utopia.

Properties of a utopia:

_____

_____

_____

Imagine that you were given space on four billboards along a highway. If you were given complete freedom, what would you put on them? After you have decided, fill in the spaces provided in Figure 12-2 with your ideas.

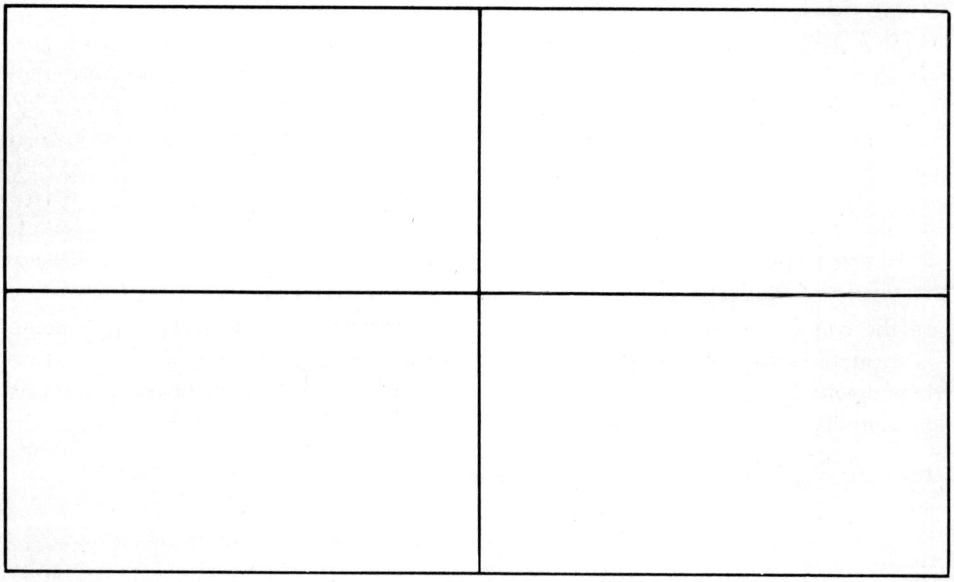

Figure 12-2

GROUP DISCUSSIONS

1. Imagining yourself a member of the *opposite* sex, answer the following questions in groups of four or five.

    a. What would you want to look like (hair, facial features, shape, etc.)?

    b. What would you like your personality to project?

    c. How would you dress—sexy or conservative?

    d. What would your attitude be toward sex, motherhood or fatherhood, and woman's liberation or male chauvinism?

    e. What would you consider your biggest problem: your attitude toward sex, the establishment of a personality, keeping up appearances, finding a career, or finding a companion?

    f. What kind of car would you drive? Would this differ from the car you would drive as your own sex?

    g. What profession would you seek?

    h. Where would you prefer to go on a date?

    i. At what age would you expect to become mature? How would this be manifested?

2. Scientists predict that someday it may be genetically possible to arrest the aging process and keep people "young" indefinitely. Assuming that this is true, answer the following questions:

    a. Would this be an acceptable practice?

    b. Could this practice become a part of the cold war with Russia?

    c. If this practice were acceptable, would there have to be a limit placed on each person's life span?

    d. How would population control be effected?

    e. How would this practice affect social patterns—economics, marriage, dating, employment, recreation, government, schools, and family life?

    f. If a limit were placed on a life span, how would each individual be prepared for death? Would the person grow old or die "young"?

EXCUSES

In the course of your life, you have made countless excuses—some valid, some fabricated. In the following exercise, you will by given the chance to demonstrate how creative your excuses can be by writing an excuse for each of the situations presented.

1. To someone you like: Why you must break a date with him or her.

    _____

    _____

_____

_____

_____

2.   To someone you don't like or would like to brush off: Why you must break a date with him or her.

_____

_____

_____

_____

3.   To your boss: Why you can't come to work today.

_____

_____

_____

_____

4.   To some unwelcome people: Why you cannot drop over on the spur of the moment—or why they cannot drop in on you.

_____

_____

_____

_____

5.   To a relative: Why you can't be with the family this year for Christmas or Thanksgiving.

_____

_____

_____

_____

_____